NO CRUSADER

Willie Walsh

No Crusader

the columba press

First published in 2016 by

the columba press

55A Spruce Avenue,
Stillorgan Industrial Park,
Blackrock, Co. Dublin

Cover design by Helene Pertl | The Columba Press
Front cover photography by Aidan Sweeney
Origination by The Columba Press
Printed by ScandBook AB, Sweden

ISBN 978 1 78218 253 5

Bible quotations from New Revised Standard Version (NRSV), New
Jerusalem Bible (NJB), Good News Bible (GNB).

Contents

Introduction

It was with mixed feelings that I undertook the task of writing this book. It wasn't that I had any compelling need to write a book but a very persistent Sales Director in the person of Michael Brennan of The Columba Press kept after me and in the end I gave in and agreed to attempt it.

Despite my initial reluctance, I have to admit that while the task was not easy, it was an enriching and, at times, a therapeutic experience. It brought me to places in my mind which I hadn't visited for more than half a lifetime.

I am grateful to all who helped me in the process of publication – the aforementioned Michael Brennan, the editor Angela Hanley, Patrick O'Donoghue, Managing Editor, The Columba Press and those who typed various sections of the manuscript.

I retired as bishop of Killaloe in August 2010 at the age of seventy-five. I welcomed my retirement and the immediate lifting of the weight of responsibilities that being a bishop entailed. I now had more time for new and old pastimes as well as being able to spend more time with my family and friends. It was lovely and I embraced it fully. Then in November 2013 I underwent a serious health setback which I thought at the time was life-ending. The grace of God, good doctors, nurses, supportive family and friends helped me through a long recovery period. The setback wasn't life-ending but it was to some degree life-changing. I found myself growing more reflective and cherishing my remaining years all the more. This book's publication owes a lot to these recent more reflective years. I offer it to a wider audience of readers in a spirit of gratefulness to God with the wish that it may help others in some small way.

There is an unwritten chapter in this book and in a sense it should be compulsory for me to write it. This chapter would consist of a long list of people's names – all those who supported me from my childhood (family) through to those who supported me during my priesthood, my years as a bishop and still support me in my retirement. People say such a chapter would only make for dull reading. It must, therefore, be taken as a given that I am indeed sincerely thankful to a great number of people.

It would be remiss of me, however, not to mention some of the people who smoothed many paths for me, during my years as a bishop in particular: my fellow priest colleagues of the diocese of Killaloe, the members of all the religious houses in the diocese – sisters, brothers, friars, monks and the many people who served on various diocesan committees as well as the people of all the parishes in the diocese. All of you have kept me in touch with reality and inspired me by your personal witness to the gospel in your own lives. Mine would have been a lonely road without you.

Willie Walsh
Ennis, January 2016

1

The Early Years

Family and farming

I remember little of my preschool years. I do have some recall of being in a pram which was raced up and down the short avenue by my brothers. I have the impression that the recognised speed limit for prams was constantly ignored but no apparent harm was done to me or the pram!

I believe my mum and dad were fairly typical parents of the time. My mum was soft-hearted and deeply religious in the traditional style. Temperamentally she seemed to tend more towards sadness than joy. She appeared to have an ear that attracted people with sad stories to tell. I think I inherited something of her softness with a similar type of ear; the tears come rolling easily, even still. My dad on the other hand presented as a strong and solid person. He too was religious but it was in a more dutiful than pious way. I think I inherited something of that dutifulness from him, especially in the area of work.

They had to have known each other since childhood because they grew up less than a mile apart in the parish of Roscrea in north Tipperary. Was it a long or a short courtship? Were they in love in their teens? There are so many details I would love to know now but back then those questions simply were not asked. Nor indeed did we ask about what part, if any, either of them played as young adults in that defining period of Irish history from the 1916 Rising, through the War of Independence, the Treaty and subsequent Civil War. I do know that my mum was a member of Cumann na mBan, but don't know how active she was in the organisation, or if indeed she was active. My dad and an uncle were involved to some degree during the Black and Tan period. I believe that, with others, they were involved in felling trees and digging trenches across the road to make travel difficult for the Tans. On one occasion, the Tans came to their house to arrest them and they escaped through the rear window. On a subsequent occasion, they took away my dad in a lorry, and gave him considerable abuse before releasing him about ten miles away. He was strongly in support of the Treaty and both Michael Collins and Kevin O'Higgins were spoken of with reverence in my home. The rest was veiled with what was referred to as 'the time of the troubles' with an unspoken message that these matters were best left in the past.

I had to go and check the records to find out when Bill Walsh and Ellen Maher married. It was January 1926 and nine years later, on 16 January 1935, Ellen gave birth to the last of her six children. Thus, I began the journey of life with five older siblings – Joe, Maura, Kitty, Eddie and John. (Joe died suddenly at the young age of fifty-five. Eddie passed away following a short illness just before his seventieth birthday). We grew up in the townland of Glenbeha, which translates as the Glen of the Beech. There were fine beech trees in the area but the glen part seems strange as it was high above the town of Roscrea, some three miles away.

The early part of my life was very much dominated by school and farming. The farm was part of a large estate bought around 1925 by a group of local farmers. They then divided it in such a way that, taking account of the land each of them already had, all of them would now have a viable holding. The portion acquired jointly by my dad and my uncle Ned was fairly large and was very good land. My dad was a good farmer who worked all the hours in the day. We farmed dry stock and milch cows. The milk was sold from a horse-drawn float in the local town of Roscrea. That was in the pre-fridge era when milk was sold house to house from the churn to the jug each day of the week. I remember the occasional excitement of being allowed to accompany my uncle on these milk rounds.

I recall my dad as a person of honesty and integrity. He was also a good judge of cattle – high praise for a farmer – and he would never engage in any form of deceit in buying or selling. We normally had a few men working on the farm – it was the labour-intensive farming era – and he always treated them with respect and paid them properly. They in turn responded generously with pride in their work. I particularly remember Tommy O'Meara as an excellent ploughman. Your skill as a ploughman was often judged by the straightness of the drills you open. Tommy never opened a crooked drill. There was Danny Hanlon who always worked as if the farm was his own. I liked working with Danny, especially in winter time, when he engaged in off-farm activities such as hanging gates, repairing roofs, building walls and even some basic plumbing and electrical work. We didn't get electrocuted but had a few close shaves! I believe that this experience gave me some skills with my hands which served me well in later life, including the capacity to repair broken hurleys. The latter I found excellent therapy in my hurling years. John Joe Flannery had spent some time as a Cistercian monk before he came to us as milkman. I suspect that the cows never before heard anyone taking milk from them as he sang 'Gloria in Excelcis Deo' and other Gregorian chants! John Joe returned to his religious calling as sacristan in Roscrea parish church in later years and often welcomed me there when I visited to celebrate Mass.

From an early age, the boys in our house participated in the work on the farm. There was great satisfaction in tasks like saving hay, cutting corn and especially the annual round of threshings, when the neighbours gathered to help each other on the day. The children were welcome to join the fun after school. The tougher jobs were thinning turnips and sowing and picking potatoes. The farm work was also a source of a little pocket money. My dad always paid us at the end of the week the amount agreed beforehand – 'after some bargaining'! I often think that the experience gave me a certain attitude to money. You earned it through hard work and you didn't squander it on things you didn't need. I don't think I am mean with money but I like to think I don't spend it foolishly.

Roles, of course, were clear in those days. My mum looked after the housework and everything in the immediate vicinity of the house – feeding the hens and other fowl and care of the garden. My dad looked after the farm. The same division of labour applied to the boys and girls. Even to this day when I visit my sisters they instinctively assume that I don't do things like cooking, washing up or ironing. I have to admit that they are probably wise in relation to the cooking!

I assume that my home was a reasonably happy one. We didn't examine such ideas in those days. It never occurred to me growing up that my home was any different from any other house in the area. Our nearest neighbours were the Kenneally family – with four girls and one boy. We grew up together, went to school together and played together. Sadly, when we went away to secondary school we gradually lost contact. It is only in later years that you begin to regret that those early and formative experiences were not allowed to develop into lifelong friendships, but they remain very happy memories.

I believe that growing up on a farm was a really enriching experience. We learned to appreciate the workings of the natural world around us. We observed the changing cycle of the seasons and how this affected the sowing, growing, maturing and harvesting of crops and how the decay of winter prepared for new growth in the spring. We became comfortable with ewes and lambs, with cows and calves, with pigs and bonhams, bullocks, horses and ponies. The natural cycle of fertilisation, pregnancy, birth, growth and death unfolded in the animal world. It still came as a surprise, though, when I began to discover that a similar cycle operated in the human world – no more finding of babies under heads of cabbage! My cousin Laurence told me recently that my older brother and he, on hearing the news of my birth, searched under every head of cabbage in the garden without any further discovery!

Primary school

I began my schooling at four years of age. I don't recall any great trauma in doing so, probably because I was with my older siblings. We went to the local Corville National School where two elderly ladies, Mrs Maher and Mrs Browne, taught. They were both gentle and kind in an era where 'spare the rod and spoil the child' was the accepted norm. Perhaps it was because my parents felt that we could do with a little more discipline that the boys in the family moved to the boys' school in Roscrea when we reached third class. The regime there was somewhat stricter and while I got slapped occasionally, I have no bad memories of primary school. I have a special grateful memory of one teacher, Diarmuid Fitzgerald, who, perhaps more than any other, gave me a love for mathematics – sums, as it was called in those days – which was to remain through my life. I later spent twenty-five years teaching maths and physics and derived much pleasure from it. Diarmuid's influence as a teacher was enhanced by the fact that, despite being a Kerryman, he played hurling for Roscrea and marked the legendary Tipperary hurler Tommy Doyle in the County Final in 1945. The match was drawn but unfortunately we lost the replay.

Some other memories of childhood are learning to play cards at a young age and later, in my teens, some all-night sessions in my uncle's house nearby playing Twenty-Five or the more risky Pontoon; developing a strong interest in hurling, spending hours after Sunday Mass playing pitch and toss on the road outside the church or going hunting rabbits during winter.

Boarding at St Flannan's

In September 1947 my brother John and I went as boarders to St Flannan's College in Ennis. We had been booked into the nearby Cistercian College but I suspect that one of the local priests, who was a regular visitor to our home, persuaded my parents to send us to St Flannan's, which was the diocesan secondary school, instead. Aren't our lives so shaped by accidents such as these – where you went to school or indeed where you went that night you met the person you went on to marry. I often asked young couples at pre-marriage courses if they ever wondered would they be with a different partner if they had gone to Tulla rather than to Sixmilebridge on that night.

Life in Flannan's in 1947 to 1952 was no holiday. I still have part of a ration book which was issued by the government during the war and which I brought with me to Flannan's. Food was sparse and rough and ready. General living conditions were not hotel-like either. We were crowded into cold dormitories where the basin and ewer were still the order of the day. Some winter mornings one had to remove the ice before washing. Chilblains were a very common ailment.

Discipline was severe – no question here of 'spare the rod'. The teaching staff comprised of about ten priests and four lay teachers. Two of the teachers – both very good teachers when judged by exam results – were very severe in their use of physical punishment. Most staff members were reasonably kind except for a dean of discipline who had the unenviable task of caning those of us who were sent to him for punishment. Each day a long line of boys awaited him outside the 'library' for their allotted strikes of a cane. I believe I would have been classified as average in the frequency of my visits there for punishment. While the overall impression was one of a harsh regime, I am satisfied that Flannan's would have been no different to most other boarding schools of the time. But what was it about boarding schools of that era? I think there was a certain macho culture, both among staff and students, which created a tension between 'them' and 'us', and any softening of that tension that might border on kindness or friendship was seen as something of a weakness. Manliness – being able to take your punishment – was highly valued. That culture may have helped 'us' to survive the battle with 'them', but it must have been torture for some students and indeed for some staff who put greater value on kindness, gentleness and mutual respect than on our rugged 'manliness'.

Despite the harshness of the boarding school regime, we survived and even enjoyed parts of it. We made friendships, some of which lasted a lifetime, and for that I will always be grateful. I am grateful too for the deep interest in hurling that I developed there, which, again, has lasted a lifetime. I do, however, sympathise with those who had no such interest and still were forced out to play games in midwinter. While I didn't fulfil my ambition to play Harty Cup hurling, many of my best memories of those five years are connected to hurling.

And so we progressed towards the Leaving Certificate and towards trying to decide what we wanted to do in life. Because of my interest in maths and physics, my mind was almost set on engineering as a career. Another thought, however, began to develop in my final year. Religion had always played a significant part in my home life – rosary every evening, serving Mass in the local church, familiarity with the various priests who worked in the parish – although perhaps reverential respect rather than familiarity would be more accurate. Religion was also central to the life of the local community. Also, in St Flannan's there was daily Mass, the rosary and other prayers. Furthermore, we had a number of visits from missionary priests telling of their lives in various countries and inviting us to consider joining them.

I have often asked myself why I eventually decided to opt for studying for priesthood. I believe that the strongest motivation had more to do with fear of losing my soul than with any noble motive. My religious experience up to that time was strongly influenced by an image of God who was 'up there' watching every detail of my life. All the wrong things I did were recorded and I would have to answer for them on the day of judgement in order to decide whether it was hell or, at best, purgatory for me. On reflection I don't think I was a top-class sinner at that time. There was, however, a very strong emphasis on sin and, in particular, on any failure in the area of sexuality. There was a belief in a judgemental God and that the threat of hell was never far away.

While the primary motivation for priesthood was not, therefore, a very selfless one, I would like to think it became more generous as the years in the seminary went by and when the salvation of others became as important to me as my own. Hopefully that motivation has developed further over the years as a loving, merciful, compassionate and forgiving God became the only God in whom I could believe. If there was some generosity in those earlier years, perhaps it is indicated in my desire to join a missionary congregation. I had been in contact with St Patrick's Missionary Society based in Kiltegan, Co. Wicklow. However, the local curate intervened again and suggested that I should apply for the home diocese of Killaloe.

Another influencing factor in deciding to study for priesthood was the expectation that a number of my class-mates would take the same route, even though we would never admit it to each other until it was finalised. Peer pressure operated in those days too. Between fifty and sixty of us sat the Leaving Certificate in St Flannan's in 1952, and around twenty began studies for priesthood the following September. I have often related those figures to young people in today's post-primary schools. Naturally, they find it hard to believe. The figures represent a totally different world in which hundreds of young people entered priesthood and religious life each year. Not only were parents supportive of their children entering priesthood and religious life but the wider community was equally supportive. I would certainly have gotten the message in my own local community at that time that the very best thing you could do with your life was to enter priesthood, and so began my journey into the unknown in September 1952 at St Patrick's College, Maynooth.

2

Studies for Priesthood

Maynooth – early impressions

In September 1952, together with some ninety other students from the various dioceses across the country, I began my studies for priesthood in St Patrick's College, Maynooth. Eight other classmates from St Flannan's began with me – Conor McNamara, Brendan McNamara, Tom Molony, Tim Frawley, Pat Sexton, John Leenane, Sean Sheedy and Louis Murphy. In total, there were close on 550 students in Maynooth, almost all studying for Irish dioceses – today's number is between sixty and seventy. At the same time there were some seventy students for the diocese of Dublin studying in Clonliffe College, with slightly smaller numbers in All Hallows College, Dublin, in Carlow, Thurles, Kilkenny, Waterford and Belfast. These colleges catered for students both for Irish dioceses and for other countries, mainly across the English-speaking world. Besides these, there were large numbers of young men in the various religious orders, congregations and missionary societies. The vast majority of these were to serve across the world in what were then called missionary countries. There were, of course, similar numbers of girls entering religious life at the same time. There were approximately 19,000 women in religious life in Ireland by mid 1960 in a wide variety of convent communities. Many other girls had emigrated and joined religious congregations elsewhere. It was a time when the Church dominated *all* aspects of our lives.

The Maynooth experience corroborated that special position of Church in Irish society. It was something of an overwhelming experience for a young man of seventeen years. The very buildings themselves spoke loudly of its stature. There was a feeling of a powerful institution which was well aware of its own importance. The college was built in the second half of the nineteenth century with the approval and support of the British government, who did not want Irish priests being educated in Europe and returning with radical ideas of revolution. The principal building was designed by Pugin and built in the Gothic style. This vastness and grandeur seemed to enhance the perception of power and importance. Even the very names given to these buildings such as Humanity, Logic, Rhetoric, Dunboyne and Stoyte House conveyed a message of self-importance. While the inner comforts did not always match the outer grandeur, it still was a considerable improvement on the sparse conditions at St Flannan's.

On entering Maynooth, I found myself as one of almost six hundred young men all journeying in the same direction. We all dressed in the same way – long black soutane and white clerical collar. We all rose in response to the bell at 6.30 a.m., prayed, ate and recreated on the same daily schedule. It was a system that had worked in Maynooth since its foundation a century and a half previously, so why change it? The goal was clear: to train young men to be good priests – dutiful and obedient in serving a tried and trusted institution that was totally confident of its own rightness.

Learning in the form of lectures and private study occupied a large section of the day. All students studied for a Bachelor of Arts or of Science as Maynooth was recognised as a constituent college of the National University. Those of us who did not take philosophy as a degree subject took some in-house lectures such as cosmology, psychology and ethics in preparation for the later study of theology.

I would have adjusted fairly easily to the Maynooth rigid regime. The regulated life probably suited me as I would have been fairly compliant with rules, accepting them as God's will for us. My image of God was still the One who must be obeyed. Again I was happy with the community-style life which facilitated the formation of strong friendships, some of which have lasted a lifetime.

If I were to find fault with the system, and this is very much in hindsight, I would say that the formation was too sheltered and too cut off from the outside world. It was a life that allowed little contact with the people whom you were preparing to serve as priests. Even during holiday time, we were expected to be somewhat apart from the friends with whom we had grown up. I still cringe a little with embarrassment when I recall during my first break from Maynooth, going to Mass on Sunday in my local church wearing a black suit, black overcoat topped off with a black hat – talk about taking myself too seriously!

Another strange aspect of Maynooth life was the formality of relationships between staff and students. We were addressed formally as mister – 'Mr Walsh of Killaloe' – and not by first name. Staff rarely spoke to you outside of class. There were a few exceptions such as the late Cardinal Tomás O'Fíaich who seemed to know every student in the college and James McConnell who lectured in mathematics and who enhanced my interest in the subject. An interest which has lasted a lifetime.

Seminary formation

There has been much talk in recent years about seminary formation. It has been suggested that the deficiencies in such formation may have been a contributory factor in the tragedy and scandal of sexual abuse. I do believe that our formation was quite limited. It was largely a question of rules which must be obeyed because these rules were an expression of the will of God for you at this time. There was little allowance for difference of character or temperament. One size fitted all; individualism was seen as a significant character defect. We were never encouraged to appreciate our own humanity. There was a suspicion that being human was dangerous. Real spirituality seemed to be the opposite of real humanity.

And what of the formation in the area of sexuality? Maynooth, and perhaps to a lesser extent Rome, gave us little formation in the area of understanding/integrating/ maturing in relation to our sexuality. One's sexuality was something that must be controlled. Any deviation in relation to sexuality was seriously sinful – purity was paramount. I do believe that the lack of good human formation in relation to sexuality left many of us ill-equipped to understand the complexities of human relationships that we encountered later in life. I certainly feel that I learned far more in this area during a couple of training courses and working with Accord than I did in Maynooth, or later in Rome.

Sexual orientation was rarely mentioned explicitly in our seminary training but what were termed 'singular friend-ships' were completely discouraged. It was only as the years went on that it dawned on me that the term 'singular friendships' was a veiled reference to homosexual friendships.

In making these comments I am not in any way being critical of or blaming the staff in these institutions. They were products of their own training and formation. It is also well to remind ourselves that the science of psychology and of human formation is relatively new. Of course, human formation is as old as humanity but the type of studied formation, which is quite common today, only began in the middle of the twentieth century. In a similar way, parenting is as old as humanity but the art of parenting only became a topic of serious study around the same period.

Irish College, Rome
At the end of three years in Maynooth, I was informed by a local priest that Bishop Rodgers wished that I would go to Rome for the study of theology. My initial reaction was one of disappointment at having to leave Maynooth, especially having to sever the bonds of friendship which had been built up over the previous three years.

The first task then in September 1955 was to actually get to Rome and this proved to be an exciting experience for a young untravelled man of twenty. These were the pre-Ryanair days! Indeed, for us students they were also the pre-Aer Lingus days. Accompanied by some older students from the college, we travelled by boat from Dun Laoghaire to Holyhead, then by train from Holyhead to London. After overnighting in London, we took a train to Dover, a boat from Dover to Calais and a train from Calais to Paris. After a night in Paris and our first encounter with French food and wine, we had a twenty-four hour train journey to Rome, breaking the trip at either Florence or Milan. Journeys to Rome usually took three or four days. Journeys home were more leisurely, stopping off at places like Venice, Vienna, Munich and Brussels. This was just ten years after World War II and there were still the ruins of that war visible across the continent, especially in Germany and indeed in Rome itself.

First impressions of Rome

If first impressions of Maynooth were of the size and grandeur of the buildings, first impressions of Rome were all the more inspiring. The magnificence of St Peter's Basilica, the richness of St Mary Major, the agelessness of St John Lateran and the resounding sounds of St Paul's Basilica were truly impressive. We arrived in Rome to the recently built Stazione Termini – Mussolini had ensured a grand entry to the city. One moved quickly from the twentieth century *stazione* to the ancient Coliseum and the Imperial Roman Forum, to the Victor Emmanuel Monument, less than one hundred years old. Rome was truly the eternal city.

Pius XII was pope – the only pope I had ever heard spoken of. The very sight of him being carried into St Peter's on the gestatorial chair by men in formal dress was awe-inspiring. Pius had been elected in 1939. He was of an aristocratic Italian family. He always appeared to me as chillingly cold and austere but at the same time awe-inspiring.

The Irish College was very different from Maynooth. It was a much smaller place with just sixty students. The smaller number allowed for a greater participation in the life of the community – in drama, debating, music and games. While the rules were very much the same as Maynooth, their application was far more relaxed. Perhaps it was again a case of Rome making the rules and expecting others but not themselves to observe them! Initially because of my own conservative nature, I found this easy approach to rules rather strange and perhaps a bit disturbing, but I got used to it and for that I am grateful. I feel that it gave me a more balanced approach to rules and regulations.

Some language difficulties

The students in the Irish College were nearly all Irish. We had a couple of Australians and Canadians. English was the daily language. However, we attended all our lectures in the nearby Lateran University, where the language was either Latin or Italian. Certainly in the early stages this caused problems, particularly in oral examinations. However, in the kindly traditions of Italians, many of the professors allowed us to answer in English – 'You are Ireland, so you may speak it in England!' – sounding both kind and amusing to our ears. It would be less than honest to say we learned as much theology as our counterparts in Maynooth, but perhaps the experience of Rome, and especially the more relaxed approach to life by the Italians themselves, made up for the deficit in theological knowledge. I feel that the Roman experience made me and others slightly freer in ourselves than the more rigid system of Maynooth would have done.

Studying in the Irish College at a time when travel wasn't as easy as today meant that we only came home every second summer. The college had a villa south of Rome in a small town called Formia. The villa was on the Mediterranean – we just had to cross the road to get to the beach. (A villa on the Mediterranean sounds impressive – it was a recently built house with about twenty-five bedrooms and an oratory, all sparsely furnished.) Holidays in Formia were leisurely and we spent hours each day swimming from a raft which we floated on tar barrels and anchored some two hundred metres from the shore. We had just two hours of study each day in addition to community spiritual exercises. The rest of the day was free. In Formia we got a first-hand view of intensive Italian agriculture, made possible by warm sunshine and the availability of an ample supply of water. Antonio and his son Cosimo farmed the acre and a half garden attached to the villa, reaping at least three crops a year. They cultivated vines, corn, tomatoes, peas and a variety of other vegetables.

One day each week was given to exploring the surrounding countryside and at the end of the holidays we had two weeks to travel around Italy. It was here that I learned the art of thumbing a lift, which has left me sympathetic to hitchhikers ever since.

From Pius XII to John XXIII

Towards the end of our second stay in Formia, news came from Rome that Pius XII was unwell. He died a month later in October 1958. Pius was the only pope I had known – I was just four years old when he was elected, so the prospect of having a different pope and all that surrounded his election was an exciting experience. The favoured ones to succeed were cardinals Agagianian, a member of the Roman Curia, and Lercaro, Archbishop of Bologna. Lercaro was seen by many as too progressive socially with some suspicion of sympathy with the Communist ideology. Bologna was then a stronghold of the Italian Communist Party. There was some mention of Montini of Milan (later Paul VI) and Roncalli, the

Patriarch of Venice. We in the Irish College were clear that Agagianian was the appropriate choice. After several trips across the city to St Peter's Square when smoke was expected, white smoke eventually emerged from the small pipe at the gable end of the Sistine Chapel.

Then followed the traditional: '*Annuncio vobis gaudium magnum, HABEMUS PAPAM, Angelo Giuseppe Cardinale Roncalli*,' who took the name John XXIII. We returned to the college quite indignant that the cardinals dared to elect this portly, happy-looking seventy-six-year-old to lead the Church! We felt that the electors had ensured that there would be no change – he would be a *papa di passagio* – a caretaker pope.

Summoning Vatican II

John XXIII was no caretaker; his papacy lasted only four years but proved to be a revolutionary one. He was a kindly convivial man with easy charm and wit and was the most loved pope of the twentieth century. He dispensed with much of the formality of his predecessors. Within three months of his election, he announced his intention to call an ecumenical council to discuss with his fellow bishops the pastoral needs of the Church. The old guard of the Vatican were outraged. Pius XII and his predecessors were clear that all important decisions were made by the pope and the task of cardinals and bishops was to carry out his instructions. If any questions arose as to how these instructions would be applied, the Roman Curia supplied the answers. The very idea that the pope would call his fellow bishops together to discuss the issues of the day bordered on the heretical! Monsignor Antonio Piolanti, a formidable member of this same Curia, lectured us in dogmatic theology. He told us that there was no need whatever for such a council and that furthermore there was a provision for the possibility of the pope losing his mind, in which case he could be removed from office. It seemed to us that poor Piolanti was in danger of losing his own mind, such was the determination with which he opposed the idea of a council!

Pope John moved ahead despite the opposition of the Curia and preparations for the Council began. The story of the Second Vatican Council is well documented elsewhere. At the time it brought new hope and new life to the Church.

Ordination and further studies

When I first entered Maynooth, the prospect of a further seven years' study seemed a lifetime. The end did eventually dawn on the 21 February 1959 in Rome, with my ordination to the priesthood. Ordination day is obviously one of the real high points in the life of a priest. It is what I had set out to achieve seven long years before. It was a high point for all our classmates and their families. All my own family, except my brother Joe, who had to look after the farm at home, made the journey to Rome for the event. I celebrated my first Mass in the Church of St Alphonsus Ligouri (founder of the Redemptorists) in Rome. The ancient, but familiar, icon of Our Lady of Perpetual Succour hangs above the main altar and has been enshrined in this location since 1499 (the church was rebuilt in the nineteenth century). My mum had a particular devotion to Our Lady of Perpetual Succour, which prompted me to choose this church for my first Mass. Looking back, I would not have seen my mother's faith and spirituality as being sophisticated enough for me, with all my theological training. I think now of her and her strong faith with a deep appreciation, as well as humility and embarrassment at the arrogance of my 'educated' youth. I recall my ordination day and how both my parents knelt to receive my first blessing, and how my training and their respect for priesthood overlooked the great blessings they had bestowed on me in a thousand ways prior to that day. Their love for one another and for me was the first blessing I received in my life.

Being assigned to a parish curacy is the normal expectation of a priest after ordination. In our diocese at the time, because of the surplus of priests, the expectation was that a newly ordained priest would work outside the diocese for anything up to ten years before getting an appointment in the diocese. When I was ordained, we had a surplus of some thirty priests, most of whom were working in England. However, that route was not for me. I was informed by Bishop Rodgers that I should return to Rome for further studies. I spent the following three years studying Church law (Canon law). One could hardly say that Church law is the most exciting of subjects but the lack of excitement was more than adequately compensated for by the new approach to the papacy taken by Pope John XXIII. He brought a whole new meaning to the office. He was no longer 'a prisoner of the Vatican' – a tradition maintained by the popes since the annexation of the Papal States in the unification of Italy in the second half of the nineteenth century. The fact that he had already summoned the Second Vatican Council added to the anticipation that we were moving towards a whole new era in the Church. Preparatory work for the Council was well under way and there was much talk of widely different positions between those who believed that there was no need for any change in the Church and those who felt that radical change was necessary.

Those of us doing postgraduate studies were free from the ordered seminarian regime and had a great opportunity to explore Italy and to learn more of Italian life. I still fondly recall one such exploration of Sicily with its extraordinary mixture of Greek, Moorish, Spanish and Norman civilisations. Through the joint efforts of four fellow students, the trip also yielded the following from Roman civilisation – if you can put an air to it!

Dublinensis in urbe ubi puellae sunt pulchrae
Ego primam videbam Mariam Malone.
Parvum currum rotabat et per vias clamabat
Emi pisces viventes, viventes vero.

Viventes vero, viventes vero
Emi pisces viventes, viventes vero.

Erat piscis mercator et quis ammiratur
Nam sic erat pater et mater primo,
Parvos currus rotabant et per vias clamabant,
Emi pisces, viventes, viventes vero.

Viventes vero, viventes vero
Emi pisces viventes, viventes vero.

De febri peribat nec quisque salvabat
Et sic erat finis Mariae Malone
Manes currum rotabit et per vias clamabit,
Emi pisces vivientes, viventes vero

Viventes vero, viventes vero
Emi pisces viventes, viventes vero

I had come to Italy from a very traditional Irish family. That traditional approach had been strengthened by the experience of St Flannan's and Maynooth. Rules were rules and must be obeyed. I am not suggesting that I always obeyed the rules, but I would never have questioned them. In Maynooth, we were often reminded that the rules were the will of God for us at this time and I always accepted that and was comfortable with it. When I went to the Irish College the rules were more or less the same as Maynooth, but the students did not seem worried about breaking them. In Maynooth if you didn't appear for Mass in the morning or indeed if you had a relaxed approach to rules, it was seen as a sign that you didn't have a vocation.

The Italians themselves had an easy attitude to rules. When it came to religion, they were perfectly confident that they were Catholic and if you pressed them a little further, they were *Cattolico, ma non fanatico*. Their approach gave me a certain freedom in regard to rules and regulations. Rules are important for good order and discipline but we must avoid the situation where rules become more important than the purpose for which they were made in the first instance or where they may be in tension with the primary value of love. I believe that this approach to rules and regulations, gained from my experience in Rome, served me well throughout my life as a priest.

My studies in Rome ended in June 1962 but the love for Italy and the Italians, for pasta and pizzas has lasted a lifetime.

3

Teaching at St Flannan's

New challenges

On returning to Ireland from Rome in the summer of 1962, I was informed that I was being appointed to a teaching post in St Flannan's College, Ennis. In order to qualify for teaching at second level, I was sent to Coláiste Éinde in Galway to study for the Higher Diploma in Education at Galway University. Coláiste Éinde was an all-Irish boarding school drawing its students mainly from Irish speaking areas of Donegal, Mayo and Galway, including the Aran Islands. Teaching in an all-Irish school was quite a challenge in that I had been out of touch with the language for some ten years and whatever Irish I learned at school was Munster Irish. The early months were difficult but gradually I became reasonably proficient in Irish. Difficult though the experience was, it gave me a new *grá* for the language which has stayed with me ever since. I also discovered that teaching was to my liking, although I confess that I was not at all happy with the quality of some of my teaching in that first year. We attended lectures at the university, given by An t-Athair Eric MacFinn, a scholarly, gentle priest from the diocese of Clonfert, who lectured in Irish from thumb-soiled notes which must have been written many years before. We managed to get through exams with the minimum of work.

I found the priests in Galway diocese very friendly and welcoming and I enjoyed good relationships with my working colleagues, both clerical and lay. I have particularly fond memories of Canon James O'Dea who was a friend of the College president, Paraic O'Laoi. James would join us for supper when he was going to meetings of the Galway County GAA Board and regularly regaled us with tales of the inner workings of the GAA.

One aspect of working in Galway which I found quite disappointing was the constant shadow cast by their bishop, Michael John Browne. Michael John was well known for his authoritarian style of leadership and he seemed to instil a sense of constant fear among many of his priests. There were regular reminders of the danger of not abiding by his rules: 'If the bishop saw you not wearing your hat … if the bishop walked in … if the bishop …' He appeared to me to be lacking in proper respect for his priests. I was happy to be able to return to Killaloe where our more kindly Bishop Rodgers posed no such threat.

Returning to St Flannan's, where I had been a student eleven years earlier, to work alongside colleagues, some of whom had been my teachers, did not pose any great problems. They either had forgotten or forgiven any troubles I had caused them as a student! They welcomed me on board and bonds of friendship formed quite quickly.

Teaching

I recall two particular events from those early weeks of teaching. The students in one class in particular seemed quite pleasant and friendly and appeared to have no objections to my efforts at imparting some knowledge of mathematics to them. My rude awakening came when the then president John Cuddy visited the class for revision. It quickly became quite clear that whatever these pleasant students had been at for the previous month, it had little to do with mathematics. I wondered for a couple of days if he would have a quiet word with the bishop suggesting that whatever talents I had might be better used in some other area of the diocese. He didn't do so; he was long enough around to know that there is no substitute for experience. The other experience was a more difficult one. Supervising or just trying to keep order in a study hall of two hundred teenagers eager to test the 'new fellow' was not an easy task. On the second night, things were getting a little out of hand when paper bullets began to strike the blackboard beside me. I bided my time until I spotted the culprit as he was about to release the elastic catapult. I have to confess I laid a heavy hand on him. I was faced with the dilemma that if I let him win there would likely be increased diversions the next night. I found it quite an upsetting experience and resolved that night to never again raise a hand to a student. I recalled the incident with that student some years later and was very pleased to discover there appeared to be no evidence of any permanent damage! I found as the years went by that if you treat students with respect and kindness, they in turn will respond generously.

The early 1960s was a good time to return to St Flannan's. Change was in the air across Europe as it began to recover from the devastation of the Second World War. Old hostilities gave way to new cooperation between the countries involved. Change was in the air in Ireland, too, as Taoiseach Seán Lemass was moving the country out of a long period of economic stagnation and protectionism, opening it up to the wider world. Irish TV started broadcasting on 31 December 1961 and further opened us to that world. Pope John XXIII was opening up the Church to renew and adapt itself to the pastoral needs of the modern world.

The St Flannan's to which I returned reflected that mood for change. The traditions built up over its eighty years of history where a president/principal made all major decisions, teachers taught, students studied and deans of discipline kept order, were beginning to be questioned. We were fortunate with our president of the time, John Cuddy, who was open to new ideas. He initiated regular staff meetings in which educational policy, school discipline and staff–student relationships were discussed. Formal parent–teacher meetings were put in place – not exactly breathtaking reforms when judged by today's standards, but forward-looking at that time.

Change is in the air
The students too were eager to involve themselves in the need for change. I refer in a later chapter to the second half of the 1960s as being the era of the angry young men. These young men had visions of changing the world and were eager to begin with St Flannan's. We had long debates inside and outside the classroom on student rights, educational policies, social philosophy and religious faith and its practice. There were times of tension between what they perceived as freedom and what we understood as good order and discipline. I believe that we as staff and they as students were enriched by these discussions. I particularly remember meeting a staff member of University College Dublin at that time. He complained to me that some of the Flannan's men

were heavily involved in every student protest in Dublin. I told him I was flattered by the complaint.

The angry young men of the sixties were replaced by the scruffy young men of the seventies whose protest, if it was protest, seemed to be expressed by denim jackets and long, unkempt hair. The series of class photographs along a school corridor tell the story of change. 1975 must have been a hungry year for barbers!

During that period, there was also the somewhat worrying phenomenon of dropouts, where a very small number of students simply ceased to take any active part in what was happening in the classroom. I suspect that some of the dropping out may have been connected with the beginning of smoking cannabis, which was starting to become available at that time. There were the usual staff discussions as to what action should be taken – talk to them, try to understand them, or tell them to 'shape up or ship out'. It is always a fine balance between what appears to be for the good of the individual and the good of the school community. Quite understandably, parents will always approve of stern measures, provided that their own child is not involved.

When I speak of angry young men and of dropouts, I am of course talking about a tiny minority. The vast majority of students of the time were quiet, hard-working and fully occupied with preparing for examinations. Like any other time, there were the ones who were not so quiet and not so hardworking; and these were characters whose presence enriched the life of the school. This tiny minority made their contribution by challenging us as staff to constantly review our own values and attitudes.

I have a sense that from the mid 1970s onwards, there was an increased emphasis on academic achievement. Reflecting the world in which they were growing up, there seemed to be more emphasis on university points and a sense of competitiveness and individualism. It was more about getting to the top of the world than changing the world. It was more about jobs and money than about justice and social cohesion. Issues which provoked ire and fire in the sixties were greeted with a shrug of the shoulders in the eighties.

During those years of teaching, priest colleagues working in parishes often suggested that I should come out into the real world in which they ministered. They were partly right in the sense that schools can be small, inward-looking worlds, in which both staff and students are singularly focused on the task of learning and preparing for examinations. But schools are also extremely important places. They are the soil in which the seeds of the future world are sown. That soil needs to be tilled and generously fertilised so that those seeds can sprout, shoot and grow to maturity. I always felt that teaching was a great privilege and a sacred vocation. It was a privilege to help to open the minds and hearts of young people to the wonder and beauty of the world and to help them to grow in confidence in themselves and in their own potential. I have no regrets that almost half my years of priesthood were spent in the classroom.

Hurling

St Flannan's had a long tradition of hurling. I was happy to have been involved in coaching the college teams with equally committed colleagues, Seamus Gardiner and Hugh O'Dowd, for many years. Winning the Harty Cup was the Holy Grail of colleges' hurling and we had a fair amount of success in that regard. Many of our players later lined out for their respective counties and some became household names in hurling lore. I hesitate to name names as they all made their own valuable contribution to our teams.

The tradition of hurling continues to the present day with significant staff involvement in coaching. Success in the form of trophies has become more elusive since the closure of the boarding school in 1995 with the consequent loss of players from the surrounding counties. However, I am satisfied that hurling is still alive and well in St Flannan's College and that it brings much enjoyment to students and staff alike.

Mixed memories

Many of those of my age have some unhappy memories of school days. I never believed that schooldays were the best days of my life and as a teacher I never had any inclination to return to the other side of the teacher's bench. I have no doubt that some students will remember St Flannan's of the sixties, seventies and eighties with more affection than others. Memories are, of course, selective. Most of us tend to remember the pleasant things and to blot out the less pleasant. For me, there are a thousand memories of those twenty-five years, memories of success and failure, memories of comedy and sometimes, alas, of tragedy. The most precious memories of all are the unspoken ones – friendships formed which have endured beyond the college walls. Those more than any others make me grateful to have been part of it all.

4

Parish Ministry

A new experience

In July 1988 I was appointed curate in Ennis parish. I was sad leaving St Flannan's, where I had been for twenty-five years. I would have been happy to continue teaching indefinitely as I very much enjoyed the work. I believe I had got on well with my teaching colleagues and the students. Besides the teaching, I was very much involved in hurling. I was also heavily involved with the Catholic Marriage Advisory Council, now Accord, in its work of providing pre-marriage courses and marriage counselling. I was also working with the Galway Regional Marriage Tribunal.

It is usual for diocesan priests to have to move from one parish to another several times in their lives. Moving is never easy. When you have spent a number of years in a parish you will have gotten to know people and relate easily to them. Then you find yourself in a new place and you have to start all over again. At least in moving to the cathedral in Ennis, I had the advantage of already knowing a lot of people in the town, including many whom I had taught in St Flannan's.

Working as a curate in Ennis parish was, however, a completely new experience and it took some time to adjust to it. As a teacher one's work is very structured. It is clear when you are working and when you have time off. Working as a priest in a busy parish is very unstructured. While there is a fixed schedule of Masses and some other recurring duties, much of the work is responding to particular pastoral needs as they occur. Two successive days are never the same. As I grew into parish pastoral work, I gradually realised that leaving teaching at the age of fifty-three was good for me. New experiences and new challenges can bring new life and new commitment to our world.

I had been working for twenty-five years mainly with young people in a school environment. I now found working with the broad spectrum of people of all ages that you find in a parish a new and very interesting experience. Some older people, especially those living alone or in poor health, can be sad and lonely but I always found them welcoming and appreciative of a visit. But many older people are just wonderfully interesting as they recall their own life experiences. Many have a deep wisdom which only life can teach. You learn to understand why wisdom, in the very best sense of that word, is so much praised in the scriptures – especially in the Old Testament.

As a curate in a parish, you experience the successes and the failures, the times of joy and the sadness in daily life. I think of the joy of parents in the new life of their child as they bring him/her for Baptism. I think of the young vibrant love of couples preparing for marriage and the old love or sometimes the renewal of love in older couples as we celebrate with them the silver and golden jubilees of their wedding. Sadly, at times you experience something of the pain of marriage break-up, and there is no marriage break-up without a lot of pain. I think also of the sadness on the death of a partner in marriage; the heartbreak of tragic deaths of young people and the devastation which always accompanies suicide. Trying to accompany families through such tragedies is one of the most difficult tasks in the life of a priest and can be quite a draining experience – all the more so if a priest is living on his own in a rural parish. It is, of course, also a real privilege to share in people's suffering and to try to accompany them on the journey towards healing or just coping.

Schools and hospitals

Visiting primary schools was another part of the parish routine. One tried to give extra time to classes preparing for First Communion and Confirmation. Working at parish level and later as bishop has certainly increased my admiration for the work of our primary school teachers. I would have always found the teachers welcoming and appreciative of a visit. I am old enough to remember that schools were not always happy places for children. I can now say that the vast majority of schools seem to be very happy places where children are treated with the respect and love to which they are entitled. Thankfully, the 'spare the rod and spoil the child' era is over, and teachers must get most of the credit for this change. I do have a strong sense of the wonderful service given by them and I am not just thinking of their contribution to handing on the faith to our children. I am thinking of all their work in preparing our children for further education, in helping them on the journey towards adult life, in giving them solid values for life and in helping to develop their talents in academic, social, artistic and sporting activities. I believe that if we ever allow the work of our teachers to be devalued, our society will pay a heavy price. I am aware that school has changed a great deal over the past twenty years. Schools are now catering for children with very diverse backgrounds in faith, culture, language, etc., and teachers have had to adapt to this diversity. They have done so remarkably well. I believe that our teachers are today playing a critical role in welcoming and integrating the children of immigrants into our society.

Regular visitation of hospitals was again a new experience for me. I still recall my first round of the wards in Ennis hospital, introducing myself to nurses and staff as the new curate in the parish. I was apprehensive that they might regard my visit as something of an intrusion into their busy workload. In fact, I found the nurses, doctors and all the hospital staff most welcoming and helpful. I was always impressed by their dedication and commitment. A society that truly values the working of our hospital staff is a society that truly cares for our sick. In more recent years, we seem to have taken wages as a measure of how we value people. Of course, adequate payment is important for everyone but it certainly should not become the only measure of how we judge the importance of the job.

Care of marriage

A very significant part of my ministry as a priest and bishop was my involvement in the care of marriage. I believe it was in 1964 that I suggested to Bishop Rodgers that we should consider having marriage preparation courses in the diocese. He agreed with the idea and, as so often happens when you make suggestions, I was given the task of arranging such courses.

The emphasis in those early courses was on information, advice and direction – none of your modern 'what do you think yourself' or 'how do you feel' stuff! When it came to sexuality, a male doctor spoke to the men and a female nurse spoke to the women. A psychiatrist always began his talk emphasising that in marriage 'man is the breadwinner and a woman's place is in the home'. Nobody protested; that was the accepted norm of the time, when female teachers and civil/public servants had to leave their jobs when they got married.

Some years later, in 1969, we established the Catholic Marriage Advisory Council (CMAC) in the diocese. CMAC (which eventually became known as Accord in Ireland) had been set up in England in the mid 1950s to offer supportive counselling to marriages which had been affected by the long absences from home of soldiers fighting in the Second World War. Gradually, it began to offer counselling to other married couples and to provide education for marriage. Centres were established in a few Irish dioceses in the 1960s. Because I had been involved in organising marriage preparation courses, I was asked by Bishop Harty to set up a CMAC centre in Ennis. The task was a fascinating experience.

Besides counselling and marriage preparation courses, CMAC also offered a service in natural family planning. When this service was launched, I was delegated to place a notice for it in the local newspaper. The following week I checked the paper but could not find the notice. I called to the office to make my complaint that they had failed to print our notice for family planning. The receptionist went to the printing room and returned with the paper pointing out where the notice was placed. There was my notice for family planning in the middle of several planning applications for houses! The receptionist didn't seem to see anything funny about the placement and I did not reveal my own amusement.

We assembled a group of volunteers. To be deemed suitable for training as counsellors they were put through a day-long, fairly rigorous selection process. The selection and subsequent training process was directed from the CMAC head office in England, and was done to professional standards. The training lasted for one year, with weekly night sessions and a number of residential weekends. Thus began a series of selection processes, training courses and work with CMAC/Accord that continued through more than forty years of my ministry.

This involvement with Accord has been one of the most enriching experiences of my life. Working on equal terms with married people gave me an appreciation of, and insight into, the area of marriage and sexuality that no seminary formation could have given. Furthermore, the people with whom I worked were more affirming of my priesthood and gave me a quality of friendship and love greater than I experienced in any other area of ministry. For that, I am deeply grateful.

It was not all plain sailing, of course. There were lots of debates and sometimes significant tensions along the way. Some of the principles on which CMAC operated came under suspicion at times by some Church authorities. The concept of non-directive counselling was new to a Church which had been very much directive. The principle of self-determination – allowing and enabling couples to make their own decisions rather than attempting to impose solutions – caused some questioning. The non-judgemental approach towards any person, no matter who they were or what they may have done, was not in keeping with the thinking of many Church people of the time.

When I was appointed bishop, I thought my association with Accord had ended, but I was then appointed as one of the bishops' representatives on the central executive. Members of Accord tend to be strong, independent-minded people, motivated by their lived experience of marriage and of non-marital relationships. They were never slow to put forward their vision for the care of marriage relationships. Bishops tend to be equally strong, especially when loyalty to the Church's understanding of marriage is at stake. It is understandable, therefore, that at times there were tensions between the two bodies. Tensions arose around issues such as the appropriateness of counselling couples whose union was not recognised by the Church, of counselling couples of other faiths, the question of non-Catholics working as Accord counsellors, the legitimacy of counsellors working with unmarried cohabiting couples and, in later years, counselling gay couples. Questions would also have arisen in relation to Accord's loyalty to the Church's teaching on family planning. Accord counsellors would generally say that you meet people where they are; you hope that by empathising with them and trying to help them in a way that is compassionate and non-directive you may help them to move towards a better place in their relationship. As a member both of the central executive of Accord and of the Bishops' Conference, I sometimes found myself sandwiched between two differing viewpoints. It wasn't always a comfortable place. Such conflicts and tensions are to be expected and I believe are a healthy sign of life on the part of such groups.

Despite any tensions, I believe that all bishops would agree that Accord has made, and continues to make, a very significant contribution to marriage and to all that marriage entails over the past half a century. I believe that the real strength of Accord and its contribution to Christian marriage lies in that it is a like-to-like ministry – married people ministering to married people – and in its rigorous selection process, together with its initial training and further in-service training.

Throughout my years of priesthood I also worked in the area of marriage tribunals with the Galway Regional Marriage Tribunal and the National Marriage Appeal Tribunal. The Church sees marriage as a sacred covenant/contract by which two people enter a lifelong relationship of love. As with all contracts, it is assumed that the contract is valid unless it can be proven that there was a substantial defect in it, which would make the contract invalid. Marriage tribunals have the task of examining a marriage which has broken down to decide if there was a substantial defect there from the beginning, which would make the marriage contract invalid.

Vatican II's document *Gaudium et Spes* (*The Church in the Modern World*) speaks of marriage as a covenant of life and love between spouses. This covenant is seen as mirroring God's covenant with his people, which is characterised by fidelity and love. For theologians and for married people, the word 'covenant' presents a richer understanding of that total commitment of life and love that is marriage than the word 'contract', which we associate more with business and commercial dealings. However, ecclesiastical jurisprudence still tends to use the word 'contract' to describe the act of entering marriage.

I would be less than honest if I were to say that I found working in this area either satisfactory or fulfilling. I did the work because the Church had put this process in place and people whose marriages had broken down felt the need to apply for a decree of nullity. It was, I believe, important to try to respond in a compassionate pastoral way to this need. It was comforting to be able to give a decree of nullity. It was heartbreaking to have to tell someone, who perhaps was already in another relationship, that the judgement of the court was the nullity of the marriage had not been proven. It felt as if this was further adding to the pain of a broken marriage.

For me, there was the deeper problem of the whole foundation of our tribunal system. Was our work a genuine upholding of our teaching that marriage is indissoluble or was this a form of what is sometimes referred to as 'divorce, Catholic style'? Certainly, in some cases I would have been perfectly satisfied that no marriage existed from the beginning. On the other hand, there were cases where three different judges might well have given a different judgement in the case. Of course, the same thing can be said of civil courts, where a different judge or jury might bring in a different judgement. I believe, however, that our response to marriage breakdown and the whole question of second unions needs a great deal more study so that we can continue to respond in a more Christ-like, compassionate way to those whose marriages have broken down and who still wish to be active participants in the life of the Church. While I am encouraged by the more open discussion on these matters at the Synod of Bishops in 2015, and by Pope Francis' recent regulations in simplifying the nullity process, I truly feel that the Church has a long way to go yet before it truly understands the complexity of marriage and relationships.

In making these comments with regard to our marriage tribunal system, I am not in any way questioning the integrity of the many people who work so generously for our tribunals. I believe that they do everything in their power to treat the people they meet in a respectful and sensitive way.

Maintenance versus renewal

There are two key aspects of work in any organisation. On the one hand, the work you are doing has to continue in relation to administration and production. On the other hand, to keep the organisation alive and vibrant, one needs to constantly try to do things better, to be open to new ideas and to let go of what is no longer necessary. Working in a parish requires that varied approach, which we might term maintenance and renewal. In many ways, maintenance is the easier of the two. It is easier to continue to do the things with which you are familiar – celebrating the sacraments, visiting schools and hospitals, doing the First Friday Communion calls to the sick and the housebound, looking after maintenance of buildings, gathering the finance required and attending the usual round of meetings at diocesan and parish level. It is easy to be so busy with these that there is little time left for any vision and planning for the future or for personal development. I felt that those of us who worked together in the Ennis parish were good at the maintenance – providing the services that we traditionally provided but were not always so good in planning for the future. One of the major challenges set out by the Second Vatican Council was that of greater involvement of the laity in the life of the local church. I believe that over the years we succeeded in encouraging parishioners to play a greater role in the parish life. It surprised us on one occasion when we tried to measure it. We found that in the region of 1,500 people actively involved themselves in the life of the parish. They were involved in the parish pastoral council, area representatives, boards of management of schools, parish choir, ministries of the Word and of the Eucharist, financial administration committee, eucharistic adoration, St Vincent de Paul Society, Legion of Mary, altar society, prayer groups, baptism teams, Apostolic Work Society, etc.

In some cases, promoting greater involvement of laity will add to the work of the priest; it can be easier to do it yourself than to have a group of people responsible for doing it. Part of the problem with us as priests is, of course, our unconscious reluctance to let go, to empower people to take responsibility for their own area of activity. We often tend to want people to do something but to do it our way. I was never good at asking people to do things but was constantly amazed at their generosity when asked. Equally, a priest should be open to people's own initiatives and not feel threatened by them.

A blessing in disguise
Though I was sad to leave teaching, it turned out to be a blessing. I feel the experience of working as a curate in a parish has been a very enriching one. Furthermore, when I was appointed bishop I was better able to identify with the work of the priests across the diocese. It would have been more difficult if I had come to that office directly from the limited experience of teaching. I continued to work in the Ennis parish until June 1994 when I was appointed coadjutor bishop of Killaloe. They say that every priest has a special feeling for his first parish. Ennis was my first parish as well as being my abode during my previous years as a teacher. It

remained my abode during my time as a bishop of the diocese and now in retirement I continue to live a happy life in Ennis. It would be remiss of me not to say that Ennis and its people have a special place in my heart.

5

From Camán to Crozier

A serious addiction

The late Paddy Duggan was a staunch member of our local Éire Óg GAA Club. Affectionately known as Duggie, he was an avid hurling man. As far as Duggie was concerned there was only one real game. Soccer, Gaelic football and 'rubby' (as Duggie called it) were all foreign games. As for golf: ''tis easy for ye hit the ball with nobody marking ye!' I visited him in hospital when he became seriously ill. On one visit he gave me the sad news: the consultant had told him that he had only weeks left to live. He asked me to celebrate his funeral Mass and I assured him that I would do so. 'That's fixed now, Willie, but I still say that we would have won that county final if they listened to me at half time.' Funeral arrangements had been made and immediately Duggie got back to the more important issue of the county final.

I wrote an article for a GAA magazine some years ago in which I suggested – tongue in cheek – that coaching hurling teams was another form of drug-taking. It is certainly addictive. It has the highs of winning and the lows of losing. You give it up regularly, deciding that you will never coach a team again. The following year someone approaches you and you inform them very clearly that you have given it up. They return within a week or two suggesting that 'you might just do a couple of sessions to start them off'. You emphasise that it will be only a couple of sessions but very quickly you are hooked again, unable to withdraw. Like Duggie, I suffered from the addiction for some thirty years.

Growing up in north Tipperary, it was hard to avoid being interested in the game. Since boyhood I have admired the skills of the game and loved that sound the sliotar makes as it meets the ash in the many twists and turns in its relationship with the hurley. There was a field beside our house at home where I played hurling with my brothers Joe, Eddie and John and our neighbouring pals whenever we got the chance. It was the field of my dreams – that one day I might line out with my native Tipperary. Such dreams were never fulfilled – no county selectors ever showed the slightest interest in me – but that never thwarted my love of the game.

I was fortunate to have many opportunities to play hurling in the local primary school in Roscrea and the secondary school in St Flannan's in Ennis. Hurling was part of the staple diet at St Flannan's – for me the most tasty part! As we studied for priesthood in Maynooth, hurling was a significant part of our leisure time activities. Later, in Rome we frightened some people on the buses as we boarded them with what seemed to be dangerous wooden weapons on our way to Campo Verano. Lest you be too impressed, Campo Verano was a local soccer pitch on which clouds of dust rose with the clash of the ash on Monday afternoons – grass was in short supply.

When I was appointed as a teacher to St Flannan's College I was involved with hurling and for some thirty years prior to my appointment as bishop, I was involved every year with some team, be it college, club or county.

A call from the Nuncio

My involvement in coaching ended in 1994 when I was appointed coadjutor bishop of Killaloe and thereby hangs a tale. At the time of my appointment I was working with Len Gaynor and Ger Loughnane as back-room team to the Clare senior hurlers. To our delight, we had beaten my native Tipperary in the first round of the championship, thus reversing our previous year's heavy defeat at their hands in the Munster final. Our defeating Tipperary was a great boost and we were quietly confident of winning the next game against Kerry. Most of our anxieties then lay in meeting Limerick in the Munster final. It is allowable in hindsight to admit that we were confident we would beat Kerry, but at the time no member of management would articulate such feelings as it would be considered detrimental to a team's training and progress that they might take the semi-final for granted. The run-up to the semi-final was an anxious and exciting time and my mind was generally preoccupied with hurling thoughts as I went about my daily busy routine in the parish of Ennis.

It was into this hectic mix of parish work and sporting activity that one day a phone call came from the Papal Nuncio in Dublin. A Papal Nuncio is the Vatican State's ambassador to a particular country but he also acts as a link between the local church and the Vatican. In particular, he has the task of assessing priests who might be deemed suitable for appointment as bishop in a diocese. How can I describe what it means to a priest to have a call from the pope's representative in Ireland? It might be similar to a newly elected politician receiving a call from the newly elected Taoiseach when he is putting together his cabinet. So when the Nuncio calls, you sit up and pay attention.

It would be disingenuous of me to suggest that I was shocked or surprised, or that this call from the Nuncio came as a bolt from the blue. I was aware that many of my priest colleagues had over the years thought of me as a possible candidate to succeed our bishop of the time, Michael Harty, who was then in his twenty-seventh year as bishop of the diocese. Michael had intimated that he was growing tired under the weight of the office and its many demands. He had asked Rome to consider appointing an auxiliary or coadjutor bishop so that he might work in tandem with him for the final years remaining to him before officially retiring at seventy-five years of age. I was led to believe that my name was listed, among others, in consultative polls of clergy and selected lay people organised by the Nuncio at regular intervals over the years even when a bishopric is not vacant.

When the telephone call came from the Nunciature, I was asked by a secretary if I would take a call from the Nuncio and naturally I agreed. I was put through to the then Nuncio, Archbishop Gerada. He simply asked me if I was free to come and see him at his residence on Thursday, 9 June. Again, I said yes and that concluded our conversation.

What thoughts went through my mind after I put down the phone? Was my heart pounding? Did I feel the excitement of an ambition about to be realised? Was I proud of myself that I was about to reach the pinnacle of a career in the Church? Did I doubt that it was about anything other than my being asked by the Nuncio to be the next bishop? Did I immediately sink to my knees in prayer and find refuge in the Lord? I confess to none of these.

Naturally, I had a strong suspicion what was on the Nuncio's mind but I too had things on my mind. I had no sooner put down the phone that I realised that we had our final training session for the Kerry game on the night of Thursday, 9 June. There was no way I was going to miss that regardless of my agreed meeting with the Nuncio. Without thinking anymore about it, I immediately rang the Nunciature and asked to be put through to the Nuncio. When he came on the line, I very courteously explained to him that I had a prior commitment for 9 June and would it suit him if I went to see him on the following Monday instead. He didn't question me as to what was more pressing for a priest than a meeting with the Nuncio and I didn't enlighten him as to my prior commitment. I felt he might not understand the importance of a final training session before a Munster semi-final. He simply agreed to meet me on the following Monday. We defeated Kerry on the Sunday and had now qualified to meet Limerick in the Munster final.

Reservations and acceptance

Meanwhile, I had the small matter of an appointment with the Papal Nuncio. I found my way to his residence on the Navan Road, Dublin. Archbishop Gerada was a friendly talkative type who seemed to have an ability to engage in a lot of what can only be described as 'small talk'. Perhaps I misjudged him and failed to see that he was only trying to put me at my ease. He soon informed me that the Holy Father wished to appoint me as coadjutor bishop of Killaloe. I hesitated in regard to accepting the appointment and I gave my reasons to the Archbishop.

Since receiving the Nuncio's invitation to meet with him, I had given serious thought, despite my other preoccupations, to some matters that I felt might hinder my acceptance of the post of bishop. I had worries in relation to some areas of

Church teaching such as family planning and the exclusion of those in second unions from the reception of the Eucharist. I made it clear to the Archbishop that I held views that might be considered at variance with the official Church position on these issues. I suggested he might wish to make further enquiries in relation to these views, though I made it clear that I was happy to discuss them with him there and then.

Of course it was to be expected that in the run-up to selecting a candidate for the office of bishop, the Holy See would have done its homework as regards a person's loyalty to Church teaching, etc. In a sense I was being cautious for fear that maybe they had overlooked to do so in my case. I made it clear to the Nuncio that while I was not a crusader on these issues, I felt bound in honesty to let him know that I had some worries in regard to the Church's position on them.

I suggested to the Nuncio that he might take some time to review the matter. If after that the Holy Father wished to revoke the decision to appoint me, then that would be fine with me and I would treat the entire matter with appropriate confidentiality. The Nuncio's response was fairly typical of any cleric responding to an expression of doubts by any member of the faithful. All of us, he said, have doubts at times and the priests of the diocese wanted me to be their next bishop and he felt that I should accept the appointment. I agreed to accept and I was informed that a public announcement regarding the appointment would be made in two weeks from that acceptance.

I find myself needing to explain my hesitancy over accepting the office of bishop on one hand, and my apparent caving in under the Nuncio's slight pressure on the other.

Why didn't I say no there and then and be done with it? I can honestly say that I had no driving ambition to high office in the Church. My driving force was a personal conviction of the truth of Christ's message of love for all and a personal commitment to preaching that message in word and deed. I raised my doubts with the Nuncio simply because I wondered if someone harbouring such doubts could be deemed suitable for the office of bishop. I was no crusader, but neither was I willing to hide my views for the sake of promotion. As far as ambition went, I was always open to whatever turn my life took insofar as it was in line with my priestly conviction to preach God's Word.

I had been aware that my colleagues, and some lay people also, believed that I had leadership qualities that marked me out as bishop material. Whilst I didn't seek the office in any way, I did see it as an honour and a privilege to be considered a suitable candidate and to be chosen as the next bishop of Killaloe in succession to Bishop Michael Harty when he retired. I assumed that that succession would be three years later when he reached seventy-five, the age at which all bishops were required to offer their resignation to the Holy See.

A bishop in waiting

So I returned to Ennis as a 'bishop in waiting' or coadjutor bishop. I was happy to have this role as it gave me ample time to learn the ropes through assisting Michael Harty in the final years of his episcopate. A coadjutor bishop assists the serving bishop and has automatic right of succession. The only other coadjutor bishop of Killaloe whom I had known was Joseph Rodgers, who had been coadjutor to the nationally known Bishop Michael Fogarty, who was bishop from 1904 to 1955. Bishop Rodgers was coadjutor from 1947 to 1955. I believe his years as coadjutor must have been quite difficult. Bishop Fogarty was over eighty years old when Joe Rodgers was appointed. As Bishop Fogarty's health declined Bishop Rodgers could do little more than await the call from Bishop's House to fill in for the ailing bishop. During those eight years, he had little defined authority or responsibility. It had to have been a very difficult apprenticeship for him before finally succeeding as bishop in 1955.

My own apprenticeship was to be very different in that Bishop Harty had actively sought a coadjutor to assist him and he seemed happy with my appointment. He also informed me that he would not be working until he reached seventy-five but would be tendering his resignation in the autumn of the following year, 1995. Between us we agreed that my ordination as coadjutor would take place in October 1994 when the hurling season would be over.

The Lord had other plans. Sadly, my hurling career ended a month later when we were well beaten by Limerick in the Munster final. The good news, of course, was that the following year Clare went on to win the Munster final and the All-Ireland for the first time in eighty-seven years. My friends weren't slow to remind me that Clare immediately won the All-Ireland when they got rid of me from the back-room team. That's what friends are for! And so ended my active hurling career, but not my interest in the game. I now sit in the stand wondering why the selectors down there cannot see the necessary match-winning moves.

But the Lord also intervened in a much more striking way. Bishop Michael died suddenly in his sleep on 8 August of that year, 1994, and I was thrown into the responsibility of acting as bishop before even being ordained. It was somewhat frightening at first but I was lucky to have the support of Fr

Gerry Kenny, the secretary at Bishop's House, who was familiar with all the routine work there. Gerry continued as secretary for most of my time as bishop and I am ever grateful for his loyal support and hard work. Indeed all who worked at Bishop's House were a great support to me. I also had an immediate sense of support and welcome from the priests and the religious of the diocese and of the people of the parish of Ennis where I had ministered for the previous six years.

Cineáltas Chríost

Soon after my appointment I was informed that I must choose a coat of arms and a motto for my episcopate. I was not enthused by the idea of a coat of arms. It sounded to me to be rather pretentious and an outdated relic of a time when princely bishops occasionally went to war with a neighbouring bishop or the civil authority. I had no intention of going to war with anyone, but not being a crusader for radical change, I decided to abide by the tradition. For the coat of arms I selected symbols of the diocese, of my native parish of Roscrea and of the parish of Ennis where I had ministered as teacher and priest for more than thirty years. I did, however, insist on the removal of the decorative hat and tassels surrounding the coat of arms.

I devoted more thought to the selection of a motto. A bishop's motto is a phrase that is meant to be a reminder of his vision or priorities, which hopefully will give direction to his pastoral care as bishop. It is intended to be something of a guiding light in your episcopate. My predecessor Michael Harty took as his motto *Caritas Super Omnia*: Charity Above All; my successor, Kieran O'Reilly, chose the words *Verbum Tuum Veritas*: Your Word is Truth. I wanted my motto to reflect in some way the kindness and compassion of Christ. After some efforts to find the appropriate phrase, Fr Seamus O'Dea, a priest of our diocese, who had a feel for the Irish language, suggested *Cineálta Chríost*. Dineen's Irish–English dictionary translates *cineáltas* as 'kindly, gentle, humane' and interestingly adds that *capall cineálta* is a 'willing horse'. I felt that I could at least measure up to the latter. I like to translate *Cineáltas Chríost* as 'the kindliness of Christ'. I was conscious that I was putting an ideal in front of me which was going to be very difficult to fulfil. I was only too well aware of my own frailties but felt that I needed something which would challenge and inspire me. I feel that *Cineáltas Chríost* did challenge and inspire me, despite the times when I failed to live up to that ideal. It is not for me to judge how I fared in being faithful to the motto *Cineáltas Chríost*. I believe that I tried to be faithful to it and am satisfied to leave any such judgment in the hands of a merciful and loving God.

On 2 October 1994, I was ordained as bishop of Killaloe in the Cathedral of SS Peter & Paul in Ennis and set out on a new phase of my journey through life. As Michael Foley, long time hurling analyst for the then *Cork Examiner*, described it: I had moved from 'Camán to Crozier'.

6

My Life as a Bishop

Early awakening

Most of us, when faced with a new and important task in life, begin with some sense of trepidation. We inevitably wonder about our ability to deal with the new responsibilities that go with it. I suspect, for example, that parents must be quite frightened when they are first faced with the responsibility of being a parent. I certainly worried about my capacity to take on the responsibility of being a bishop. I worried whether my faith was sufficiently strong. I worried about my own frailty in regard to living out the gospel values given to us by the example and teaching of Jesus Christ. I worried about my capacity to provide adequate pastoral leadership for the priests and people of the diocese. Gradually, as time goes on, such worries and fears lessen and one gets on with the task.

How do I adequately describe my life as bishop over the last decade of the twentieth century and the first decade of the twenty-first? Words like fulfilling and exhausting, joyous and heartbreaking, privilege and responsibility, loving and humbling come to mind – yes, and chaotic. All of these feelings and many more were experienced over those sixteen years. I think chaotic best describes the early months. In my eagerness to respond to every call, I found myself constantly on the go with little time to give serious thought as to what I was really about. It is so easy to get caught up in the warmth and welcome of people and the busyness of life. I was beginning to think that I was doing very well and the task was not as difficult as expected and then reality suddenly came knocking. That reality check came to me in two forms. There was the awful reality of having to deal with the issue of child sexual abuse. I describe the difficulties faced in this area in Chapter 7. Suffice it to say here that responding to this issue was the single most difficult and worrying task of my sixteen years as bishop. The second awakening call came in the shape of a letter from a parish priest. I was aware that he was admitted to hospital some months before for an operation. His letter pointed out to me that he had been in hospital for some three months and I hadn't visited him nor lifted a phone to enquire about his welfare. He suggested that this neglect was entirely at variance with the public commitment I had made on the day of my ordination as bishop, that the care, support and love for the priests of the diocese would be my first priority. He added that I had taken as my motto *Cineáltas Chríost* but he had not experienced any *cineáltas* from me since he became ill. His letter stung me; criticism which you know is quite justified always stings. I replied immediately, accepting his criticism and apologising for my neglect. I thanked him for his honesty and promised that I hoped never to be guilty of such lack of care again. I have always been grateful to that priest. He could have continued to give out about me rather than giving out to me. I believe that I did make it a priority from then onwards to regularly visit priests who were ill or retired.

Criticism such as this helps to bring a little order to life, to distinguish between what is important and what is not important, what is urgent and not urgent. One needs to say 'no' at times, otherwise life can become chaotic and those who shout loudest are the ones who get heard and attended to.

Administration versus people

Another battle goes on in a bishop's life. It is the battle between administration and being with people. So many people in positions of responsibility are faced with this difficulty in today's world. Paperwork has multiplied and it is often easier to get tied to a desk than to be out among people, attending in a real way to their pastoral care. It is often much easier to write a formal response to an issue than to go and sit down with people and talk with them. Talking is always the better way to resolve difficulties.

As time went on, I feel I grew into the job and became more comfortable with it. I can honestly say that I was as happy and at times as unhappy with life over those sixteen years as at any other stage in my life. I found nearly all of the work joyful and fulfilling. Yes, some of it was terrible and some of it heartbreaking but I found I could cope, even with heartbreak, when I was satisfied that I had responded in the proper way. What was more energy-sapping and discouraging were the times when I was simply not sure if I had acted in the right way.

Relationship with priests

The Second Vatican Council opened up a new vision of Church for many of my generation. It was a Church that was more understanding, compassionate and willing to engage with the human in trying to make the kingdom of God a lived experience. It inspired me at the time and I believe continued to inspire me during my ministry as bishop. The Council decree concerning the pastoral office of bishops in the Church (*Christus Dominus*) sees the role of bishops in terms of both the Universal Church and their own dioceses. In regard to the relationship between bishop and priests of a diocese the Council document states:

> His priests who assume part of his [bishop's] duties and concerns ... should be the objects of his particular affection. He should regard them as sons and friends ... always be ready to listen to them and cultivate an atmosphere of easy familiarity with them, thus facilitating the pastoral work of the entire diocese. Bishops should be solicitous for the welfare – spiritual, intellectual and material – of their priests (*Christus Dominus*, n. 16).

In 2003, Pope John Paul II reiterated much of the above sentiment in his apostolic exhortation *Pastores Gregis* and gives it a more contemporary tone:

> The Bishop will always strive to relate to his priests as a father and a brother who loves them, listens to them and welcomes them, corrects them, supports them, seeks their cooperation, and as much as possible, is concerned for their human, spiritual and material welfare (n. 47).

In many ways these two quotations say all that needs to be said of the relationship between bishop and priest. They certainly set out the ideal in regard to that relationship. Like all ideals, there is always something of a struggle in trying to put them into practice in the daily life of a diocese. Support, mutual welfare and fraternal correction are the foundation of the bishop–priest relationship.

My experience comes from a background of sixteen years as bishop and, naturally, I tend to see the relationship through the eyes of a bishop. I did, of course, experience more than thirty years of the reverse relationship as priest to bishop. I was fortunate to serve under two bishops who were basically kind and considerate and were not, despite the times, cut from the authoritarian cloth. The first bishop, Joseph Rodgers, participated in the Second Vatican Council. The second bishop, Michael Harty, was very committed to the implementation of the vision of the Council. While we were blessed in both of them, I often say in hindsight that they did not impinge very much on our lives. The paths of bishop and priests do not cross as much as people might think. Priests go about their daily work in a parish and the bishop–priest relationship exists within an environment of limited contact.

With regard to the father and son aspect of the relationship, some theologians suggest that it has its origins in the spiritual relationship of God the Father and the Son. I would have felt a little uncomfortable about seeing myself in that relationship with my colleague priests. I preferred to see myself as a colleague or brother priest who has a special leadership responsibility towards them and with them. However rich the father–son analogy may be, it is not the only way of describing the relationship. In contemporary terms, we could just as easily describe it as a relationship of deep respect between two people with a common goal and purpose in life.

The relationship exists at two levels – the one-to-one level and the group level. Both are important and the relationship is incomplete if one level is preferred to another. This means that bishop and priest engage with the relationship, work on it and nurture it. The Council speaks of the mutual support when it says:

> To ensure an increasingly effective apostolate, the bishop should be willing to engage in dialogue with his priests, individually and collectively, not merely occasionally but if possible regularly (*Christus Dominus*, n. 28).

On a practical level, I tried to facilitate that mutual support by having an open door and direct phone line policy to all priests. A priest should feel that he can have direct access to his bishop at all times. I believe that a bishop should also arrange to meet each priest individually every couple of years. I set out to have such meetings with each priest every two years. While I didn't always manage to keep to that schedule, I felt that such meetings were always of benefit to me and, I hope, to the priests.

I feel that support for one another is something that must be shared by bishop and priest. The bishop is but one person among many priests, which may result in the relationship making too heavy a demand on the bishop. It is important, therefore, that priests support one another. In this regard smaller groups of priests with shared interests and who look out for each other can be a very effective mutual support system. As a younger priest, I belonged to such a group for many years. We used to meet once a month in each other's houses to discuss Sunday homilies and other pastoral issues and enjoy one another's company. These meetings helped to form bonds of friendship which have endured through the years.

In more recent years, parishes have been clustered in most

Irish dioceses. While there has been some justifiable criticism of clustering as a short-term solution to the problem of ageing priests, I believe that, when implemented with consultation and in a collaborative way, it has much to offer both priests and people. I was encouraged to hear that, when asked recently what was the most important support they had, a group of priests in our own diocese overwhelmingly agreed that it was the experience of clustering and the mutual support it offered.

I pointed out earlier that the bishop–priest relationship is a dual one – the one-to-one relationship and the relationship of bishop to the body of priests. In this relationship, the bishop offers support to priests as teacher, leader, inspirer and motivator – at least that is the ideal. In this group interaction he will share with the priests his vision for the diocese and suggest some strategies by which he feels this vision may be put into practice. He will need to listen to their views and take account of them as well as extending this spirit of collaboration to include not only priests but also the laity, so that a shared vision for the diocese may be created. In 2003/2004 a listening process was organised across the diocese of Killaloe with a view to drawing up a detailed pastoral plan. It is easy to draw up a plan but its implementation is another matter. We carried out a review of the plan after a few years. We found that most parishes had made a fairly good effort at implementation but the progress was not very even. I have always regarded myself as being weak on the follow-up of such plans. I was generally very reluctant to call in a priest who was doing little to implement any proposed strategy; but I am satisfied that most our priests made a reasonable effort to try to meet the objectives of our pastoral plan.

Again, the question of care for the priests' welfare operates at both personal and group level. It is a two-way process and the welfare of the bishop should not be overlooked by either himself or the priests. In this sense he, once again, unites with the body of diocesan priests and works in cooperation with them towards their mutual welfare. A bishop can effectively address many welfare issues in, through and with the collective body of priests. As their spiritual leader, he needs to engage in meaningful consultation with them on a range of issues, be they human, spiritual, ministerial or financial. The principal vehicle of consultation is the diocesan council of priests. Again, it is very important that any decisions taken are implemented and acted upon.

A bishop needs to actively promote a variety of initiatives that assist the ongoing formation of priests, such as diocesan retreats, days of recollection, pilgrimages, formation and study days, social gatherings and sabbaticals. Attendance at such activities helps to build up bonds of friendship between priests and to promote a sense of unity and purpose to a shared diocesan apostolate. I found that attendance at such activities by priests was uneven. On occasions I have suggested to priests that if they were employees of a commercial firm, attendance at training days would be mandatory.

I modestly make the claim that I was better and more sensitive about the welfare of individual priests than I was about the body of priests. In this area of caring for individual priests I would always have placed a lot of importance on appointments of priests to a parish or other specific duties within the diocese or indeed outside the diocese. I always found the annual diocesan appointments one of the most difficult tasks facing me as bishop. The objective is to appoint priests suited to the particular needs of various parishes. I always believed that an appointment with which the priest is happy is very much at the heart of a priest's welfare and a crucial factor in the bishop–priest relationship. While the final decision in regard to a priest's appointment must rest with the bishop, consultation has to take into account the needs of a particular parish, the overall needs of the diocese, the strengths and the weaknesses of a priest and his suitability for the particular parish. Over the years as bishop I would have found this consultation process very time-consuming. I feel, however, that it was never time wasted. If a priest feels he has been sufficiently consulted and listened to and his reservations addressed, it is more than likely that he will accede to the judgment of the bishop even when initially unhappy about the proposed appointment. I see no purpose in appointing a priest to any position where he has reasonable objections to it. My own experience in this area is that getting agreement on a series of appointments is difficult with or without consultation. However, if genuine and meaningful consultation is part of the process, it will foster a good relationship between bishop and priest.

No bishop wants conflict between himself and a priest, nor does any priest want to be in conflict with his bishop. The reality, however, is that whenever people are working closely together, it is inevitable there will be occasional tensions. The source of such tension will vary from a priest feeling he has been unfairly treated by his bishop, to a bishop believing that a priest has treated a parishioner or a fellow priest in an unacceptable manner. It may be that the bishop feels that a priest is not fulfilling his pastoral responsibilities. I always dreaded having to call in a priest or visit him in his home to challenge him in regard to some action or actions which I deemed unacceptable. In spite of my fears, I can honestly say that I almost always came away from such meetings greatly relieved. Having put my case to the priest and given him an opportunity to reply, we nearly always resolved our difficulties. Dealing with any such issue in a mature, non-confrontational way can improve and give new life to a relationship. The obedience promised by a priest to his bishop at ordination will be all the more authentic and sincere if there is an open and honest relationship between them. Obedience exacted by the power of authority alone will not make for a healthy relationship between bishop and priest.

Sometimes efforts at 'fraternal correction' can end in failure. A priest may feel that a bishop is more ready to listen to those with complaints against him than to the priest himself. I may have been perceived as less than fair in this regard as I feel that a priest should be willing to go the extra mile in resolving a dispute with a parishioner. But even in situations where a priest feels he has not been treated fairly, the bishop needs to be careful not to allow a particular issue to dominate the overall relationship. Even if a priest is reluctant to accept correction in regard to a specific issue, this does not and should not detract from all the good work that he may be doing in other areas of pastoral activity.

The complexity of the relationship between bishop and priest cannot be dealt with in terms of rules and regulations alone. Priests at ordination promise obedience to their bishop. I like to think that that obedience is less about implementing in detail every direction from the bishop and more about bishop and priest working together to respond appropriately and generously to the pastoral needs of those whom it is our common vocation to serve.

As yet un-weathered by life

With my parents on ordination day

Ordination day, February 1959, Rome

Family photo, ordination day, 1959

Primary school group, 1946

Picnic in Sicily, 1961. Willie Walsh, Martin O'Riordan, Denis O'Callaghan
and Michael Olden

Killaloe students in Irish College, Rome, 1956.
Tony Cahir, Cathal Jordan, Willie Walsh,
Enda Burke

With Michael O'Carroll at Coláiste Éinde,
Gallaimh, 1963

Cusack Park, Ennis with Ger Loughnane and Len Gaynor, 1992

Enjoying a hurling match with Seamus Gardiner and Kevin O'Callaghan

Celebrating the Eucharist at the Grotto in Lourdes

With my cousin Dom Laurence Walsh OCSO, Cistercian Abbey, Roscrea

A surfeit of meetings

In my early years as bishop my domestic needs were taken care of by a very kind elderly lady called Mary Walsh (no relation), long since gone to her eternal reward. Mary had already cared for my predecessor, Bishop Harty, for more than twenty years. It was understandable, therefore, that she felt she needed to keep this new 'younger' incumbent of sixty years of age from doing foolish things! Mary was of the old tradition – bishops were in charge and priests and laity should obey. She often chided me: 'You are not going to another meeting! I don't know what ye be doing at all those meetings. Talk I suppose.' I always enjoyed her forthrightness.

For a period in 2003/2004, when we were preparing the pastoral plan for the diocese, we had a series of meetings in my house at 8.00 a.m. so that people could go to work at 9.00 a.m. When we emerged from the final meeting, which lasted from 8.00 a.m. to 11.00 a.m., Mary greeted me with, 'The United Nations wouldn't be sitting as long as ye!' Yes, Mary, and one of the great pleasures of retirement is the absence of meetings. The schedule of meetings for a bishop is endless – meetings of the priests' council, cluster meetings, meetings of the diocesan trust, meetings in relation to safeguarding children, liturgy meetings, finance meetings, catechetics meetings, priest formation days, meetings of bishops' commissions and agencies and the longest of all meetings – Bishops' Conference meetings. The Bishops' Conference, a gathering of all the Irish bishops, meets formally four times a year, twice for three-day meetings, and twice for two-day meetings. The agenda for each meeting is lengthy, dealing with a wide variety of pastoral issues.

These meetings normally begin at 9.30 a.m. and end at

5.30 p.m. There are subcommittee meetings after supper, so inevitably some heads, including my own, were inclined to drop off to sleep, especially in the afternoons. On occasions I had the experience of being nudged awake to be told that a bishop colleague had asked a question to which I was supposed to have the answer. 'Would you repeat the question please? I didn't quite hear it' didn't fool anybody. I recall that at my very first such meetings a colleague commented to me in the middle of the afternoon, 'Willie, they are not always as exciting as this.' There is no denying that at times the meetings were less than exciting. The Bishops' Conference has more than forty commissions or agencies, each dealing with specific pastoral areas. These commissions/agencies would normally have two or three bishops attached to them, together with other priests and lay people. These would meet several times a year, thus further adding to the number of meetings to attend.

Yes, Mary was right. A lot of talk goes on at meetings and often they end with talk. But many of them also lead to action and to important action. Gone are the days when bishops were thought to have all the answers and that people were simply expected to obey. The model of Church changed at Vatican II from a top-down church to a people's church and meetings are an expression of that new model.

Out and about with people
I found that one of the most rewarding and encouraging aspects of my life as a bishop was being out and about with people. There were a variety of opportunities for doing that throughout my sixteen years as bishop: administering the sacrament of Confirmation, visiting schools, blessings of new

schools or extensions to existing schools, meeting up with various committees, celebrating priests' ordinations, jubilees and funerals, attending functions, games and a variety of other activities. The biggest problem always was how to answer as many calls as time permitted.

Often we as bishops are accused of living in ivory towers. I never had any sense of living in an ivory tower. I had enough close friends who would very quickly bring me down to reality if I ever tried to climb the proverbial ivory tower! I did on occasion suggest to journalists that they might examine the circle of people in which they move. I suspect that they meet with a much smaller cross section of people than bishops do in the course of any given week.

In particular, I would have regarded the annual round of Confirmations as a good pastoral opportunity to touch the lives of people. By celebrating the sacrament over weekends – Friday, Saturday and Sundays – it gave the extended families an opportunity to attend and to share a meal together. I saw it as an opportunity to meet people, many of whom would not be regular churchgoers. As celebrant, I tried to use the occasion to impress on children how special and sacred each one of them is and to lead them from there to treat each other with love, joy, peace, patience, kindness, gentleness, faithfulness and self-control – the fruits of the Holy Spirit. I would have said little enough to parents because I am satisfied that parents hear more of what you say to their children than of what you might say directly to them. I also saw it as an opportunity to meet with teachers and to affirm them not only in their generous work in preparing children for sacraments but also for their work in preparing them for further education and in guiding them on their journey towards adulthood.

There are many questions in relation to Confirmation as we have it at present. There are questions in relation to timing: should it be given earlier as a Sacrament of Initiation or should it be looked on as sacrament of entry to adulthood? There are questions in relation to preparation: should the local parish community play a greater role through meetings of parents, faith friends and special liturgies and much more is being done in recent years in this area. There is a perception that Confirmation is often the occasion of exiting from churchgoing. The exiting may happen at this time but the sacrament does not cause it. There are a variety of contributing causes, not least of which is the pre-teen/early teenager starting to push the limits of the boundaries that had previously been set for them.

Any occasion where there is an opportunity to chat at leisure with people, share a cup of tea in the local hall, sit with people at a meal, talk with and listen to people at meetings, or whatever be the occasion, is an opportunity for a bishop and indeed for all of us to touch each other's lives. There is still, especially in rural Ireland and in our smaller towns, a sense of community and an abundance of such opportunities. The kind word, the gentle enquiry, the affirming phrase is never wasted and each such encounter is truly sacred.

Ecumenism

I grew up in a community in which there were significant numbers of the Church of Ireland people, with smaller numbers of Methodists and Presbyterians. While there were no difficulties between us when we were dealing with farming and other business matters, there was a considerable division between us when it came to worship, education, cultural and social/recreational affairs. And there were major difficulties in relation to inter-church marriages. The 1907 *Ne Temere* decree of Pius X discouraged Catholics from entering marriage with members of other churches. In the event of such a marriage taking place, the Catholic spouse had to sign a promise that all children born of such a union would be baptised and brought up as Catholic and that they would do their best to persuade their spouse to become a Catholic. Specific permission from the local bishop was required for an inter-church marriage and it had to take place in a Catholic Church, with the Catholic priest officiating.

I believe that these regulations had a very significant bearing on social interaction between the different communities. I recently had a long chat with a Protestant man of my own age. We grew up within a mile of each other but never had a real chat before. He agreed that the fear of an inter-church marriage was largely responsible for our separate social activities. A Protestant boy or girl often had to leave their own community and family if they wanted to marry a Catholic. I would have felt that our position gave little consideration to the religious convictions of the Protestant spouse. The *Ne Temere* decree was replaced by a more relaxed document, *Matrimonia Mixta*, in 1970.

A short time after my ordination as bishop, I gave a talk during Christian Unity Week in which I recognised the significant hurt caused by the *Ne Temere* decree, and expressed regret for such hurt. I received quite a number of letters from people who had been hurt precisely in this way over the years. I also received a great deal of criticism on the basis that I was causing confusion and being disloyal to the teaching of our Church.

Thankfully, the relationship between the churches had gradually improved over the years since Vatican II and there had been some easing in the applications of the *Matrimonia Mixta* document. The Catholic spouse was simply asked to do his/her best to bring up the children as Catholic.

In 1996, Bishop Edward Darling of the Church of Ireland and I set up a committee to draw up agreed guidelines on the pastoral care of inter-church marriages. During the drafting, I consulted with some bishop colleagues and other people involved in inter-church dialogue. I tried to take on board their comments, both positive and negative. In the final document, we recognised the hurt caused in the past and expressed regret for the pain caused to couples and their respective families by the lack of cooperation between the churches. The document emphasised our shared vision of the sacredness of Christian marriage, while at the same time recognising the difference which separates us.

The Congregation for the Doctrine of the Faith was unhappy with the guidelines. It was their view that we should be discouraging inter-church marriage because of the difficulties which are likely to occur in marriages when the two people are not of the same faith. They felt that it was undermining the obligation of the Catholic spouse to raise the children as Catholics. They suggested that we were blurring the truth in regard to the different positions of both churches.

I was disappointed with their response to the guidelines. I accepted that there may have been some ambivalence in our approach to the differences between the churches. I felt quite strongly, however, that all of us had an obligation to try to heal past hurts and ease the tensions between our respective churches. I was particularly conscious that this obligation was all the more acute when viewed against what was happening at that very time in Northern Ireland, where religious differences were contributing to, or at least a factor in, the awful devastation and death happening there.

I have no illusions that our guidelines on the pastoral care of inter-church marriages were somehow a major step forward on the journey of ecumenism. I believe, however, that our document at least helped further enhance the good relationships between the ministers of both churches, and thus minimise any misunderstanding between the couples themselves. If it achieved that, I believe the effort was worthwhile.

My Traveller neighbours

The deaths of ten people from two Traveller families at the halting site in Carrickmines in October 2015 shocked the country. One can only add one's voice to the sympathy and concern that so many people expressed for those two families at the time. This awful tragedy brought the whole issue of Traveller accommodation back into focus nationally. For me, it brought back memories of my own involvement in this area over my years as priest and bishop. I recall on three different occasions when caravans were destroyed by fire on the front lawn of the house where I lived as bishop. Thankfully, there was no loss of life on any of those occasions but it was traumatic for the people involved.

I can recall the days when Travellers lived in small canvas tents on the roadside and when Traveller tinsmiths visited our home offering their services in mending pots, pans and buckets. They provided a necessary and welcome service to many a household back then. As a priest, I found myself becoming more interested in their plight and in the work being done by a small but very committed group of people in Ennis working on their behalf. In my early years as bishop, the problem of parking Traveller caravans became more acute as local councils passed by-laws making such parking illegal in urban areas. As a result, Traveller families were finding themselves constantly being ordered by Gardaí to move on. In some cases caravans were impounded, even when there was no alternative place for them to go.

In an effort to give temporary relief to the tensions arising from an increasingly contentious issue, I allowed eleven Traveller families to move onto the lawn in front of my house. They remained there for about a year and a half with smaller numbers coming and going in the subsequent years. They did their best under difficult circumstances to keep the place in reasonable shape and the local council facilitated in providing waste services.

Their presence certainly brought new life around the house, with about fifty people in constant movement around what had always been a patch of well-trimmed grass. It was satisfying too to see so many children enjoying a safe place to play. There were colourful days when a marquee was erected on the lawn and a white limousine arrived with bride and groom for their wedding reception. There were amusing aspects too. Mary Walsh who kept house for me welcomed the idea of allowing Travellers to park on the lawn. She was quite sympathetic to their plight and related very well to them. She did, however, draw the line at her beloved dog, Brownie, associating with his counterparts on the lawn! Yes, there were some difficulties too. Not all of my neighbours approved of what was happening and at least one had a very reasonable complaint when some clothes from her clothesline appeared on a newly erected line on my lawn.

Where are we now with the Traveller issue? Sadly, I believe we are not in a good place. It is a very complex and difficult social issue and there are no simple short-term solutions. From my own limited experience, I offer the following observations:

- We as settled people have something of a patronising attitude towards Travellers and we need to work towards ridding ourselves of that prejudice. Every human person, no matter who they are, needs to be respected and is entitled to that respect. I believe that Travellers are often deeply hurt by the lack of respect we show to them and as a result they sometimes respond by not respecting us. Our respect for them is often conditional; and implicit in our thinking is the attitude that we don't have a problem with Travellers, provided they behave as we expect them to behave.

- A small number of Travellers do not help the situation by their anti-social behaviour. Some have been involved in serious inter-Traveller violent clashes. I have been told by Travellers themselves that much of this violence has been related to the supply and sale of drugs. The behaviour of a few has done significant damage to the majority of Travellers who are trying to live decent lives. I believe that the only hope of curbing this violence has to come from leadership within the Travelling community.

- Local authorities have a major role to play, especially in the provision of appropriate accommodation for Travellers. This will have to be done in consultation with both the local settled community and the Traveller community. The tragedy at Carrickmines will hopefully serve to ensure that safety standards at all halting sites will be improved. In fairness to our own Clare Local Authority, they have done well in this regard over the years, despite the difficulties that always arise when the location of a halting site is designated.

It is hard to be optimistic about the matter, but if we take our Christianity seriously we are challenged to continue to work towards a solution that is founded on mutual respect, on justice and on love.

A strained relationship

One of the less happy aspects of my time as bishop was the constant strained relationship I had with some of the congregations in Rome. I had told the Papal Nuncio, Archbishop Gerada, when he informed me that the Pope wished to appoint me as coadjutor bishop of Killaloe, that I had some doubts in relation to certain aspects of Church teaching but that I was not a crusader in relation to them. While I made no promise to him about altering my views, I did not anticipate that these difficulties were going to impinge so greatly on my life over the following sixteen years.

I always took my responsibility as bishop to be loyal to Church teaching very seriously and, despite my doubts, I never expressed dissent from any of that teaching. I did, however, on a number of occasions ask for further discussion and/or examination in regard to some areas of teaching in relation to family planning, the exclusion of people in second unions from reception of some sacraments, the role of women in the Church and regulation in relation to inter-church marriages. Some Vatican authorities saw this calling for discussion as dissent from, or being disloyal to, Church teaching. They insisted that the primary duty of a bishop was to preach and teach the official teaching and not to express doubts or raise questions in relation to any such teaching or its application to the lives of people.

Certainly, in the early years, I found it rather intimidating to be called before the cardinal heads of Congregations (Roman Curia departments in the Vatican) and told that I was acting in a manner which was in conflict with my responsibilities as bishop. I felt that they saw me as an inexperienced bishop from a small diocese in the west of Ireland who required correction by a higher authority in Rome. I am not someone who is so confident of his own views not to have been worried about these events. As the years went on, I felt less intimidated because I began to see that we were operating from two different theologies: it appeared to me that the officials in the Congregation saw themselves as sharing in the authority of the Pope and acting on his behalf; I felt that they were failing to respect the autonomy of a bishop in his own diocese.

A further issue arose in these difficulties with the Vatican authorities. They were insistent that our discussions should be wrapped in a cloak of secrecy. I gradually began to feel that part of this obsession with secrecy is really part of a system of control. While I had no wish to publicise our disagreements, I did feel, as we have learned to our cost in recent years, that such a culture of secrecy has not served us well.

I have no wish to provoke controversy in relation to this matter or to justify my own actions. I accept that these Vatican officials believed that they were doing what they saw as their duty. I hold no brief for any bishop or priest who uses the pulpit to preach dissent from the teaching of the Church. That is not the place for it. Speaking or writing in the public domain, where people have the right of reply, is the appropriate place for such expression. I also believe that attempts to suppress or paralyse expressions of doubt on questions relating to such teachings in the public domain, is not in the best interests of honesty or truth.

I believe that Pope Francis is working to change that whole culture of secrecy and has also affirmed the authority of each individual bishop in relation to the pastoral care of the people in his own diocese.

7

Tragedy and Shame

Early hopes

I still remember at the time of my ordination as bishop hoping that I would never have to deal with a case of child sexual abuse in our diocese. How naïve of me! Little did I anticipate that this very issue was going to be the single most painful and distressing reality I would have to deal with over the next sixteen years.

I was fortunate that prior to my appointment I had some appreciation of the seriousness of the issue. I had read some of the material being published in the United States at the time – there was very little being published in Ireland during that same period. Of course, I always knew that sexual exploitation of any other person, especially a minor, was seriously sinful. But this reading gave me a much better understanding of the terrible long-term effects of abuse on the survivor and of the real danger that any such abuser would likely abuse again.

I was also fortunate that at the very first bishops' meeting that I attended in October 1994 we had before us draft guidelines on how to respond to allegations of child sexual abuse by priests.

Sixteen years: distress and privilege

Within weeks of my ordination as bishop I received the first allegation of abuse, and over the next sixteen years I was to receive close on sixty such allegations. The majority of these related to priests of our diocese, most of whom were already dead. Some related to priests and religious not from the diocese, while some related to lay offenders.

Over those sixteen years as bishop, no task proved as distressing, no task occupied so much time as the task of responding to these allegations of abuse. It involved well over a thousand meetings with individual survivors and with advisory groups devoted to the tasks of investigating allegations, liaising with Gardaí and HSE – trying to help survivors towards healing, and putting in place procedures so as to ensure, as far as humanly possible, that such abuse would never occur again.

Over these sixteen years, every single meeting of bishops at national level devoted significant time to the abuse issue and we had a number of meetings where child sexual abuse was the only item on the agenda. At one such meeting we were addressed by a priest psychologist from the United States, who told us that the Church in the United States had already been through this tragic period and now that the issue was opening up in Ireland, it was going to take us some years to get through it. He got it wrong on both accounts: the issue of abuse was going to become even greater in the United States; and it was going to take a lot more years for us in Ireland to deal with it and there still is a lot more to be done to respond to the pain of survivors.

Work continues to improve the response to survivors, in training priests and people at parish level to ensure that agreed procedures to improve safeguarding policies continue to be implemented. All of this work is supervised by the National Board for Safeguarding Children. This board, while set up and financed by the Bishops' Conference, acts independently from it. It has shown that independence in its public criticism and challenging of some dioceses and religious orders where they found any breaches of safeguarding policies and procedures. It was, for example, that board's report to the Minister for Justice that led to the setting up of the investigation into practices in the diocese of Cloyne in March 2009. (The report was published in 2011.)

Dealing with the issue of child sexual abuse was truly distressing and painful. It was also at times a lonely place to be. Despite the fact that from the beginning I had a most supportive advisory board and later a child protection committee, very often survivors wanted to speak only to the bishop and I felt I should respect that wish. Time and again I sat in my room and listened to survivors' stories and to their pain and their anger. On numerous occasions after such meetings I sat in my room alone and allowed the tears to flow. I can honestly say that I cried more in those sixteen years than I cried in the sixty years before becoming bishop. It was distressing and painful and at all times humbling to listen to a survivor's pain. My response then and always is to try to help in any way possible towards healing.

And when I say that it was distressing, painful and at times lonely, I am deeply conscious that the greatest distress, pain and loneliness belong to the survivors. I always had members of our support group to whom I could talk on the day following a meeting while the survivor often had to go home alone in his/her own pain. My temporary pain was miniscule compared to their often lifelong pain. I was also conscious of the deep distress and at times the terrible regrets of parents of abused children. They often felt guilty that they had not noticed the danger to which their child had been exposed and thus in some way had failed to protect their child.

It was, of course, also distressing and painful to have to tell a priest colleague with whom you had worked that he must step aside from ministry on receiving an allegation, and more painful still to later tell him that his priesthood was ended. Can I risk saying that every abuser has his own story? Some were abused themselves as children; others had early experiences which in some way made it difficult for them to develop into sexually mature adults. I often asked myself the question: if I had their experience in childhood or in later years could I be in their position now? Of course sexual abuse of children is a heinous crime and every effort, including appropriate civil and ecclesiastical punishment, must be applied in order to ensure the safeguarding of children. But part of that safeguarding demands that we try to understand why abuse occurs in order to protect children at all times.

Every bishop that I know has a real abhorrence of any form of child sexual abuse. They regard such abuse as criminal and seriously sinful. There were earlier warnings of the seriousness of this issue but we failed to learn from them. Some of us were reared in a culture which had little understanding of the nature of abuse or of the serious damage done to the victim of abuse. Some would have believed that calling in the priest abuser and giving him a good telling off or sending him to a psychiatrist would prevent reoccurrence of abuse. Many were trained in a culture where the Church must be protected from scandal and what is good for the Church is good for the people. Has that view of things been seen elsewhere? What is good for the party is good for the country? What is good for our organisation is good for those whom we serve? We in Church leadership had to learn that protection of children, and not the protection of the Church, is paramount. We had to learn that our guidelines should be the example and teaching of Jesus Christ and not protection of the Church. These remarks are not in any way an attempt to excuse what happened. What happened was shocking, it was wrong; it caused unspeakable pain to so many innocent children and in some cases destroyed their lives.

Shocking reports

During the 1990s and early 2000s, the subject of child sexual abuse was a constant topic in the media. Within weeks of my ordination the revelation that Fr Brendan Smyth had abused very many children in a variety of places in Ireland received widespread publicity. The delay in processing his extradition to Northern Ireland put significant pressure on the then Taoiseach Albert Reynolds to resign from office. A number of television programmes such as *Cardinal Secrets* and *Suing the Pope* pressurised the government into setting up commissions of inquiry into the issue of clerical sex abuse. These inquiries resulted in the Ryan Report into Abuse of Children in Institutions (2004), The Ferns Report (2005), the Murphy (Dublin) Report (2009), the Cloyne Report (2011), all four of which were deeply shocking. They were shocking not only in the scale of abuse but also in the failure of Church leadership, in the form of bishops and religious superiors, to respond appropriately to the allegations of abuse. Each report tore at the very foundations of a Church which placed such emphasis on the virtue of chastity and preached a God of compassion and healing for those who are hurt.

When we seemed to be recovering from the shock of earlier reports, the Cloyne Report hit like a tsunami. At least after Ferns, Ryan and Murphy we could honestly say that these failures were in the past and that we now had guidelines in place and safeguards to ensure, as far as humanly possible, these abuses would not happen again. In 2008, Patsy McGarry wrote a very critical article in *The Irish Times* on our handling of the abuse issue. I wrote a letter to him arguing that the article was very unfair by implying that we were still not following our own guidelines. He telephoned me to say that he was satisfied that his criticism was merited and that he had reason to believe that all the agreed procedures were not being followed in every diocese. Obviously, I could not challenge him after the Cloyne Report. I think what was particularly devastating about the Cloyne Report was that it gave further credence to the assumption that we as bishops had learned nothing and to the probability that other dioceses were still engaged in cover-ups in this area. I believe that this report, even more than others, caused very serious distress and anger among those Catholics who still wanted to remain loyal to their Church but wanted the Church to deal with the issue of abuse in an appropriate manner.

The anger following the publication of the Cloyne Report in July 2011 was palpable and it was given a strong voice by Taoiseach Enda Kenny in Dáil Éireann. He was understandably severely critical of the failure of the authorities of the Cloyne diocese to respond appropriately to the allegations of child sexual abuse. He referred to the previous Ryan and Murphy reports. His most trenchant criticism, however, was reserved for the Vatican authorities: 'because for the first time in this country a report on child sexual abuse exposes an attempt by the Holy See to frustrate an enquiry in a sovereign democratic republic ... In doing so the report excavates the dysfunction, disconnection and elitism that dominates the Vatican to this day.' Strong words indeed, but I felt unable to dissent.

Some in our Church felt his speech was far too harsh. I did not share that feeling at the time and having listened to it again in a less emotional mood, I still believe that his criticism was reasonable. Furthermore, the Taoiseach recognised the work that had been done by the Bishops' National Board for Safeguarding Children. He also recognised the pain of good priests up and down the country and he did not hesitate to criticise the failures of the HSE and the Department of Justice.

I sensed a real sadness and some disillusionment among a lot of our priests at this time. Previously, many of them would have been quite critical of us bishops in that they felt that we were overly severe in our immediate standing down of priests on receipt of allegations before any adequate investigation had been carried out. I think they were now angry with us for having failed to take these very same steps. They somehow felt trapped between feeling all the pain and shame attached to the issue and being powerless to do anything about it.

Role of the media
Dealing with media during all that period proved very difficult at times. If you refused to comment there was a feeling that you were involved in some sort of cover-up. If you agreed to comment you ran the risk of saying something that might cause further hurt to survivors. I have particular memories of one such interview which I did with *Morning Ireland* a few days after the Murphy Report. I had done an

interview with Today FM with which I was happy and went almost immediately into one with *Morning Ireland*. I was asked about a colleague who had been mentioned in the report. I clearly wanted to say that he should be given an opportunity to explain his position and that there should not be a rush to judgment. For some reason I failed to make the point adequately and was then asked if I had read the report. I said I hadn't and, instead of explaining that though I hadn't read the full report I *had* read the material relevant to this particular issue, I panicked and used the unfortunate and inappropriate phrase 'looking for a head on a plate'. The media reaction to the interview was very hostile. On the days that followed there were literally hundreds of severely critical emails and phone calls, with many bordering on the hateful. It was a very chastening experience.

When I mention the media I have to acknowledge that they played a vital role in bringing the issue of child sexual abuse into the open. In doing so, they have done the Church a valuable service. Their criticisms were often very painful. But however painful it is to hear and accept the whole truth, it is always preferable to more comforting, self-deluding half-truths.

Towards healing

Bringing healing to survivors of sexual abuse is very difficult and complex. It is scarcely ever possible to bring complete healing to a survivor. No apologies, no counselling, no compensation, no matter how large, can be regarded as adequate. One cannot put a price on the lifelong effects of child sexual abuse. What helps one survivor can have the very opposite effect on another – hence the need for great sensitivity from anyone who is trying to help with healing. Any survivor will tell you that the first, most important step on the journey towards healing is to be listened to sympathetically and to be believed. In my own experience, most of the survivors that I met were revealing their story for the first time, having carried that secret and the burden of guilt that so often accompanies it for twenty, forty, fifty years.

It may surprise some who are unfamiliar with this issue that I speak of the burden of guilt carried by a survivor of abuse. Sadly, the reality is that the vast majority of survivors did feel in some way guilty, having a sense that they were partly responsible for what had happened. I tried always to reassure them that the total responsibility for abuse lay with the abuser. While such reassurance may help, they often need much more intensive counselling to help fully release them from that burden of guilt. In my experience, counselling is the single most effective instrument on the journey towards healing. Such counselling, of course, must be done by people who are highly skilled in this specific area. While proper professional qualifications are essential for such counsellors, they also need additional specific training to deal adequately with this most complex issue.

The question of financial compensation would have arisen in many instances. I am satisfied that the suggestion that some survivors are only interested in financial compensation is both deeply offensive to survivors and is quite untrue. Yes, in a small number of cases I was unhappy with the emphasis on compensation alone and with the total dismissal of counselling. Financial compensation is important, but adding any conditions – such as secrecy – to the receipt of such compensation is both unwise and ineffective and is likely to be interpreted as a further attempt to cover up. In my experience, the first and most important need of any survivor was to be listened to and to be believed. Some were told by the abuser that this was a special secret between them and that even if they did reveal it they would not be believed and they lived with that fear of not being believed for years.

I would like to add some further comments in relation to healing and I do so with caution lest I give offence to survivors who have not only lost their trust in the Church but have been damaged in their faith in God. I would never ask a survivor to forgive his/her abuser. Forgiveness is a journey, a long journey and one that is very personal. A victim of sexual abuse retains the right to forgive or not forgive his or her abuser. You are no less a Christian if your hurt is so great that it impedes your journey towards forgiveness. Forgiveness is a process that takes time and there is no measuring of that time and no one has the right to demand forgiveness from another. Likewise, the Catholic Church in Ireland and worldwide must learn to be forever humbled by the tragedy and shame of clerical child sexual abuse.

~~~ 8 ~~~

Pilgrimage of Reconciliation

Being reconciled to one another
Being reconciled to God and to one another are two facets of forgiveness. Wherever human beings interact with each other it is inevitable that at times they will hurt each other. That hurt can vary from the almost trivial, such as forgetting to return a phone call, to something quite serious, such as a deliberate personal injury. Any deliberate and unjustifiable hurt caused to another is morally wrong and therefore sinful. The wrongdoer has an obligation to try and undo the hurt caused by seeking forgiveness from God and from the person to whom the wrong was done.

It seems that we find it easier to ask forgiveness from God than from the person to whom we have done wrong. It is not always easy to approach the person whom we have hurt and to ask for forgiveness. We fear that our approach may be rejected. It is, of course, important for the person who has been hurt to be willing to forgive. This is not always easy, especially if the hurt has been a deep one. But if we are unable to forgive we are really allowing the person who has hurt us to continue that hurt. In the case of deep hurt it may be unfair to ask for immediate forgiveness. We might be able to ask the person if he/she could begin the journey of forgiveness. Forgiveness of deeper hurts is rarely instantaneous; it is rather a journey that may take some time.

Being reconciled to oneself

We have been taught to see reconciliation in terms of being reconciled to God and to each other. I would suggest that there is a third aspect of reconciliation: being reconciled to ourselves. Many of us in today's world suffer from a sense of alienation from ourselves. That sense of alienation from oneself can have a variety of causes. It can be rooted in low self-esteem or in a sense of not being valued by others. It can be rooted in things which have gone wrong in our lives – in our job, in marriage and in other relationships. It can be rooted in a permanent sense of guilt, or in being unable to forgive ourselves for wrongs done. There also appears to be a lot of unacknowledged anger bubbling just below the surface, often without obvious cause. There is also justifiable anger, which can be destructive if not properly directed. There is an angst among us that seems to prevent us from enjoying life and being grateful for the day.

I have no expertise in psychology or psychiatry but I feel that one of the challenges for many of us in today's Western world is to be reconciled to ourselves, to be satisfied to be who I am. I am not talking about being smug and comfortable with *where* I am. We all need to strive to be better people, and to contribute to make the world a better place for others. We need to strive to be more generous, compassionate and loving. I am talking about accepting our own goodness and giftedness but also recognising and accepting our own limitations and at times our own failures and sinfulness. I am, of course, very mindful that there are people who carry enormous burdens which make it very difficult for them to accept where they are – parents devastated through loss of a child, tragic death of a loved one, permanent ill health, etc. But for those of us who are not so burdened, we seldom take time to enjoy the present moment.

I am reluctant to suggest that faith or religion is a cure for all such angst – many religious people still suffer the same unfulfilled search for serenity. Yet I believe that within all of us there is a search for meaning and purpose in our lives, without which any temporary relief from the tedium of life will fail to satisfy. Augustine's 'thou hast made us for thyself, O Lord, and we will never rest until we rest in thee' is at times used to attempt to heal too many wounds which may require other therapy; however, it emphasises that only God can ultimately satisfy our deepest needs. We are not gods; we are limited human beings on a journey which we hope will lead to a final destination in God's enfolding love. Until that final destination is reached, we remain with a yearning that can never be satisfied by worldly acquisitions or possessions. We need to recognise and accept that all is not, and will never be, perfect on this pilgrimage with our fellow humans toward that end. We need to be reconciled to ourselves.

The three aspects of reconciliation – being reconciled to God, to others and to ourselves – are mirrored in the commandment of love. We are invited to love God, and to love our neighbour as ourselves. Perhaps our training has not always encouraged us to love ourselves. When we fail to be faithful to this commandment of love, we are invited to be reconciled to God, to our neighbour and to ourselves.

Being reconciled with Church

I don't know if it is a personal or a well-founded feeling that as Church, or perhaps as those in positions of leadership in the Church, we should be regularly asking for forgiveness for our sinfulness, for the hurts we have caused over the years. We have apologised and asked for forgiveness for the scandals revealed in recent years and should continue to do so.

But we need to continue to recognise the hurts we have done to a variety of people over the years. I believe, at times, we have abused our power in the manner in which we have excluded people – those of homosexual orientation, couples in second marriages, people who did not accept our detailed moral obligations. We have placed heavy burdens on people who were not always able to carry these burdens. People don't expect us to be perfect; they can cope with our failures, but they also expect, and are entitled to expect, that we treat them with respect and not talk down to them from on high. With them, we are fellow pilgrims on a journey towards God, struggling with all the weaknesses common to humankind. It was with something of that sense of the need for reconciliation that in our diocese of Killaloe we set out on a pilgrimage of reconciliation in preparation for the new millennium.

The Pilgrimage

Early in 1999, we got a committee together to make recommendations as to how we might prepare to celebrate entry into the new millennium. We had in mind celebration at both diocesan and parish level. There was a growing consensus amongst us that we needed, in some of our celebrations, to reflect the issues that were seriously impacting the Church in Ireland at that time. One such issue was the increasing revelations in regard to clerical child sexual abuse. We were conscious that enormous hurt had been caused. We needed to acknowledge that hurt and to ask for forgiveness, in so far as those who had been hurt would be able to forgive. We also decided that it was an appropriate time to acknowledge that all of us, at times, cause hurt to others and that we needed to be reconciled to each other. We agreed that all of us needed to ask God's forgiveness for our failures. Eventually we agreed that our principal celebration for entry to the new millennium would take the form of what we titled 'A Pilgrimage of Reconciliation'. The pilgrimage would take the form of a walk across the diocese from Loop Head in the west, to Kinnitty in the east, a distance of around 200 kilometres. The details of the route were worked out so that we would take in as many parishes as possible.

We sent a short letter to every house in the diocese outlining the purpose of the pilgrimage and inviting the people from the various parishes to join us on the way. We explained that the purpose of the pilgrimage was:

- to acknowledge and to ask for forgiveness from anyone who had been abused physically, emotionally, sexually or spiritually by anyone who belonged to our Church.

- to ask for forgiveness from anyone we had personally hurt and to ask those who had been hurt to forgive as far as they felt able to do so.

- to invite people to join us in a service of reconciliation in the evenings in each parish.

Just prior to the start of the pilgrimage, a skilled carpenter, John Joe McMahon from Maghera, Caher, Co. Clare, presented me with a timber crozier made from ash. This plain crozier, a shepherd's crook, was made especially for the pilgrimage by John Joe (now, sadly, deceased). Its simplicity appealed to me greatly, and I used it throughout the pilgrimage and for all liturgies thereafter.

The pilgrimage began in a small church in Kilbaha in west Clare on a cold, dark December evening. The local parish had a very creative and inspiring liturgy arranged. The theme of the liturgy was that of moving away from the hurts, the disappointments of the past and moving into the new light of the twenty-first century. It began with an elder relating to the children the story of the Little Ark. Some 150 years earlier, the people of the area wanted to build a church. The local landlords' agent refused to give them the small plot of land required for the building. They then built the 'Little Ark', which is a very small timber house still preserved in the local church. The Little Ark was placed on the foreshore each Sunday at the time when the tide was out. The people gathered on the strand while the priest celebrated Mass in the Little Ark. This arrangement continued for some years until they were finally allowed to build the church. The second part of the liturgy consisted of putting away the darkness, the hurts, the burdens, the tragedies and the wrongs done in the past and so to walk in the light of the new millennium. It was quite a moving and inspiring ceremony.

The following morning the walking began after Mass in the local Church of Cross. I still remember the sense of apprehension and anticipation. Would people join in the pilgrimage or would they see it as an ill-conceived and foolish exercise? Would they see it as an honest expression of sorrow for hurts and wrongs of the past and an asking for forgiveness or would they see it as a superficial publicity-seeking act? We honestly didn't know, but we as a committee felt the risk was worth taking. The parish of Cross/Kilbaha is quite small with a population of about five hundred people. Following Mass, around 250 people began to walk with us from Cross towards Kilkee. We stopped at Moveen School, where the local people had prepared soup and sandwiches for us.

We stayed for about an hour, which gave us the opportunity to relax and chat before we set out for Kilkee, arriving there as darkness was falling. Later in the evening we had a large gathering for a service of reconciliation with a group of local priests giving an opportunity to receive the sacrament. We knew at the end of that first day the pilgrimage was meaningful for people and our anxiety was over. The pattern of morning Mass, walking some distance, stopping for food and rest, walking again with a final liturgy of reconciliation later in the evening continued for some twenty days.

I found the pilgrimage an extraordinary experience. There was something special about simply walking with people in the wind, the rain and the darkness of December days – we even had a little snow on occasion. Walking with each other is a statement of equality, of sharing, of a common struggle with life. There is no place for pretence or for dishonesty. I feel I learned more about people, about their struggles, their sheer goodness and generosity during that twenty-day pilgrimage than I learned in any other similar period of my life.

I heard many stories during those twenty days – stories of joy and sorrow, of success and failure, stories of hurt caused by Church, and people associated with Church, going back years. I heard, too, of stories of the goodness and kindness of priests and people supporting them in difficult times. I was told a story of serious hurt caused to a family by priests and a bishop some seventy years previously, relating to the Church acquiring a piece of their property. Despite their continued loyalty to the Church and continued friendship with the local priests, the family continued to carry this deep hurt to that day. I visited the family that night and chatted with them about the issue. Eventually, after some further meetings, we agreed on a solution which I believe brought some healing and closure to the hurt caused. Were there stories of abuse by clergy? Yes, sadly there were. But very much part of the purpose of the pilgrimage was to create an atmosphere that would give confidence to people that if they wished to tell any such story they would be listened to with sensitivity and kindness.

I believe that thousands of other stories were told and listened to over those days of walking together. Over the twenty days, crowds between thirty and several hundred walked together across the diocese. Some 1,500 people walked the final journey from Shinrone to Roscrea and a similar number awaited us in the parish church when we arrived there, somewhat stiff and tired from the long journey, but happy that we had shared in a significant spiritual happening. Christmas 1999 was truly a blessed Christmas for all of us involved and gave us renewed hope as we entered the new millennium.

~9~

Eight Popes: Some Personal Impressions

During the eighty years of my life, eight popes occupied the See of Peter. Pius XI died in 1939 when I was only four years old; therefore, the first pope that I became aware of was his successor Pius XII. Growing up in a strong Catholic environment, as I did, the pope was always spoken of with great reverence. I learned in school that Christ was the invisible head of the Church and that the pope was the visible head and therefore was the Vicar of Christ on earth.

It was with a deep sense of awe and reverence, therefore, when shortly after I arrived in Rome in 1955, I first saw Pope Pius XII being carried through the central aisle in St Peter's Basilica. He was seated on the gestatorial chair borne by six gentlemen in formal dress. My impression was of a saintly, gaunt, distant figure almost beyond the human. During our student days we often went to St Peter's Square on a Sunday at noon to see him recite the Angelus and give his blessing at the window of the papal apartment. We also attended ceremonies in St Peter's where he presided at the Eucharist. The deep reverence for the pope continued throughout our student days. It would appear that in his latter days Pius XII was a lonely, anxious man attended regularly by his highly unorthodox physician called Galeazzi-Lisi, who prescribed unusual and unapproved medicines.

When Pius XII died in October 1958, we students shared in the excitement of our first experience of the election of a new pope. I have recalled in an earlier chapter our surprise on the election of Pope John XXIII. He had an extraordinary impact on the Church. He was a huge contrast to the previous two popes. He came across as deeply human, and to the chagrin of many in the Curia, he convoked the Second Vatican Council. I had already returned to work in Ireland when he died and, therefore, had little first-hand impressions of his successor Pope Paul VI. He, of course, continued the work of the Council and that is his finest legacy. He had contributed significantly to the first session of the Council prior to his election as pope, and managed to steer some of the most revolutionary documents through the remaining sessions without having a serious schism.

We tend to attribute the revolutionary work of the Council to Pope John XXIII because he had summoned it and had overseen the opening session. In fact, the first session had made little real progress, with angry clashes between those who insisted that there was no need for any changes and those who were equally convinced that there was such a need. It fell to Pope Paul VI to insist that the work of the Council continue – some strong voices would have been happy to have it brought to a swift conclusion. Paul VI managed to retain openness to new ideas and pastoral initiatives and, eventually, to steer through the most revolutionary documents on all the principal issues of the time. His later years must have been extremely difficult because of the very controversial reaction to his encyclical *Humanae Vitae*, which reasserted the traditional teaching of the Church in relation to sexuality and family planning.

The all too short twenty-three days of the papacy of his successor Cardinal Albino Luciani, Patriarch of Venice, was too brief to make any significant impression. That said, Pope John Paul I gave the impression of being a warm, gentle, humble and saintly man. His election was a surprise but the late Cardinal Hume of Westminster made a significant comment about the election of John Paul I that is worth repeating here:

> Seldom have I had such an experience of the presence of God ... I am not one for whom the dictates of the Spirit are self evident. I am slightly hard boiled on that ... but for me he was God's candidate.

We can only speculate as to what graces a longer papacy of John Paul I might have bestowed on the Church. There has been much questioning about his sudden death and the possibility of foul play. I have never read anything that convinced me that there was any solid ground for such speculation.

Cardinal Karol Wojtyla, Archbishop of Cracow, was elected successor to John Paul I. Taking the name John Paul II, he was the first non-Italian pope in more than four hundred years and the first ever Polish pope. At fifty-eight and in vigorous health he brought new energy and charisma to the office as he travelled across the world. Those of us who are old enough will remember his visit to Ireland in 1979 when he brought the country to a joyous standstill for three days. We recall his 'young people of Ireland, I love you' and our joyous response – even from those of us not so young – singing 'he's got the whole world in his hands' when he was at Galway racecourse. We remember, too, in his Dundalk visit, his poignant appeal to the men of violence to give way to peace.

Pope John Paul II presented as a man vigorous in mind and body. He was a very strong advocate of human rights in relation to freedom of religion and in regard to justice and poverty. His advocacy is credited with the downfall of communism in his native Poland and indeed for sowing the seeds that led to the undermining of communism throughout the Soviet Union. He was equally strong in his convictions in relation to the traditional teachings of the Church and was severe in regard to any dissent from, or questioning of, that teaching. This, I believe, had a significant effect in some theological institutes. Reports in some Catholic publications have suggested that many lecturers felt uncomfortable about the kind of open discussion on areas of moral teaching which would be normal in the teaching environment.

The world was shocked in May 1981 when a Turkish gunman, Mehmet Ali Ağca, shot John Paul II twice as he moved among pilgrims in St Peter's Square. It took him some time to recover from this near-death experience. He subsequently pardoned his would-be assassin and visited him in prison. He made a reasonably good recovery and continued his extensive travelling across the world. His strong stature was recognised by *Time* magazine's nomination of him as 'Person of the Year' in 1994, the person who most strongly influenced the world in that year.

In later years, his health deteriorated when he developed Parkinson's disease. His movement became slow and his voice deteriorated, but he continued to do all that his health allowed. He died on 2 April 2005 after a prolonged illness. I met with John Paul II on three occasions. Two of those meetings occurred towards the end of his pontificate, when his health was deteriorating. In 1999, on the occasion of an *Ad Limina* visit with the Irish bishops, we had lunch with him and met him for individual one-to-one meetings. The individual meetings lasted no more than eight to ten minutes. He was but a shadow of the vigorous and charismatic young pope who had visited Ireland in 1979. It was difficult to engage with him beyond answering his few enquiries as to the location of one's diocese and its key pastoral issues. His health didn't allow him to engage any further. Yet, he still gave the impression of a man intent on guiding the Church and guiding it in his way, despite the ill health.

I had the privilege of concelebrating Mass with him in his private chapel in Castel Gandolfo on the morning of 11 September 2001. After Mass I had a very brief meeting with him, simply introducing myself and four friends who were with me. Later, we spent the morning in a carefree and joyful mood wandering around the local town savouring the experience. Our joy was short-lived, however. As we arrived back to Rome in the early afternoon, we heard the horrifying news of the planes crashing into the Twin Towers. We spent a sombre evening looking at the devastation of 9/11 on television. Two sharply contrasting experiences in the space of a few hours; experiences that will forever be associated in my mind.

Cardinal Josef Ratzinger, prior to being elected Pope Benedict XVI, had the reputation of being a scholarly but conservative theologian who dealt severely with any theologian who might dissent from, or indeed question, any Church teaching. He had been head of the Congregation for the Doctrine of the Faith, formerly known as the Holy Office. He had sometimes been referred to, jokingly, as 'God's Rottweiler'. As pope, he continued to oversee a Church which was not open to any challenge or re-examination of its doctrinal or moral teaching. My reading of him is that of a man deeply committed to his personal faith, as well as one who took his role as leader of the collective faith of our Church very seriously indeed. He presented as a man driven by the duty to preserve the integrity of the traditional teaching. As a result, many would have seen him as inflexible and unfeeling with too much head and too little heart. He was certainly a man of deeply held conviction with the personal courage to stand by these convictions in the face of any opposition. I am satisfied, however, that his courage and his emphasis on orthodoxy were not oblivious to the pain and suffering sometimes caused by Church teaching.

I met with him on two occasions. The first was a twenty minute one-to-one meeting during the *Ad Limina* visit of the Irish bishops in October 2006. I was somewhat apprehensive about meeting with Pope Benedict for the first time in private. I had had my own difficulties with the Roman Curia over the years and I expected that he would have that information before him. However, I felt that I had to be honest with him about these issues – hence my apprehensions. He immediately put me at my ease and I very quickly found myself speaking about the pain of people who wanted to be loyal to the Church but who found themselves living at variance with Church teaching in some areas. I instanced people in non-sacramental unions being unable to receive Communion and people who felt unable to follow Church teaching in regard to family planning. He didn't suggest that we might look again at our teaching, nor did I expect him to do so, but I certainly got the impression of a man who was aware of their pain. He spoke of how we must try to better explain our teaching as opposed to any insistence on obedience. I was happy that he was taking the more positive 'we must explain' rather than 'they must obey' approach. I came away from that meeting much relieved and encouraged, whereas a less sympathetic man would have left me downhearted and deflated. He came across to me as a gentle, warm and humble saintly man.

My second meeting with him in the company of my colleague bishops was a much sadder one. We had been invited, or perhaps, summoned to Rome to discuss the issue of child sexual abuse in February of 2010 in the aftermath of the Ryan and Murphy reports. The meeting was attended by about ten of the cardinal heads of Congregations and by Pope Benedict himself. Each one of us was invited to speak on the matter and to make any suggestions we felt would ensure the safeguarding of children. We found many of the Roman cardinals quite defensive and reluctant to believe that the whole Church, including the Vatican, and not just the Irish Church had to accept responsibility for the tragedy. Pope Benedict attended each day but did not preside and made few interventions. It was very clear from his participation in that meeting how deeply he felt the pain of survivors of abuse and that their healing was far more important than any protection of the Church. Again, standing around and chatting with him during coffee breaks, he presented as a shy, humble man, deeply saddened by the whole tragedy. An unfortunate aspect of that meeting was our appearing on television in all our episcopal regalia when something less regal and akin to sack cloth and ashes might have suited us better. I was relieved the morning after the meeting had ended to be able to take a flight to Mombasa in Kenya to join with a group of people from our own diocese who were building a school for blind and partially sighted children. Painting walls and planting shrubs was much easier than facing the justified anger and outrage that many people expressed at our manner of dress and which was also taken up by the Irish media.

Benedict's final act as pope was to announce his own resignation. In doing so he said:

In today's world, subject to so many rapid changes and shaken by questions of deep relevance for the life of faith, in order to govern the bark of St Peter and proclaim the Gospel, both strength of mind and body are necessary, strength which in the last few months has deteriorated in me to the extent that I have had to recognise my incapacity to adequately fulfil the ministry entrusted to me.

It was a very personal and very human statement of a man facing up to the struggle of life and the overwhelming demands of high office and admitting the reality that neither his mind nor his body were any longer up to the demands being made upon them. The decision to resign was also a very courageous one, and something that no pope had done in over four hundred years. His resignation was by no means an opting out but rather a sensible making way for someone who would have the necessary strength at his disposal to carry the burdens of such an onerous office.

The first sighting of Cardinal Jorge Mario Bergoglio in the person of Pope Francis was reassuring. Fr Ronan Drury of Maynooth, in a rare editorial intervention in *The Furrow* magazine, spoke aptly of it:

A brief appearance on a balcony, a few words and blessing, not a basis, it could be said, for approval and prediction. Yet it is surely significant that the words that figure most often in comment on his first appearance were 'humble', 'simple', and 'human'. Significant too, surely, is that the new Pope's first words were a simple 'good evening' and that he ended by wishing everyone a good night's rest. Humble, simple, human. Most significant though, is that before his first blessing as successor of the chief apostle he asked the people of Rome to ask God to bless him (*The Furrow*, April 2013, p. 195).

Pope Francis has continued as he began, presenting as a humble, simple, human person. That humility and simplicity, however, combines with a courageous and indeed passionate pursuit of his own deeply held convictions. In two short years he has reminded us that our mission in life is about trying to live by the example and teaching of Jesus Christ. He speaks of a Church that must reach out to all, especially the poor, the powerless, to those whose lives may be in conflict with the ideals or even the teachings of Church. He hasn't changed any teachings but he presents them in a warmer and kinder manner – non-judgemental and in keeping with the Christian values of mercy and love. His comments on the issue of homosexuality received much publicity: 'If someone is gay and searches for the Lord and has good will, who am I to judge?' Likewise, that way he has spoken about our over-emphasis on single issues such as abortion, contraception and gay marriage is far more nuanced than what we have been accustomed to hearing from Church authorities.

There appears to be a freedom about this man, a freedom which all of us seek, but few of us find and enjoy. Certainly, few of us attain that fullness of which he spoke in *Evangelii Gaudium*: 'Those who accept his offer of salvation are set free from sin, sorrow, inner emptiness and loneliness' (n. 1). Pope Francis' freedom is obviously rooted in a deep trust in a loving and merciful God. I suspect that it is further rooted in his total acceptance of himself. He strikes me as a man at peace with himself and at peace with his God. It is this peacefulness that promises to give us freedom.

I believe that many of us, especially those of us who were in positions of responsibility in the Church, did not enjoy that kind of personal freedom Pope Francis seems to enjoy. It allows him such freedom of expression. Many of us have experienced a tension between our sense of loyalty to Church teaching and what we sometimes feel in our hearts – a tension often accentuated by the insistence of a Roman Congregation that some matters, such as compulsory clerical celibacy, exclusion of people in second unions from some sacraments or the issue of family planning, are not matters for discussion. Our hearts were speaking to us of mercy, love and forgiveness but we could not always allow ourselves to bring these values or qualities to our expression of the Christian life.

As pope, he is freer than most to bring the plight of the poor to centre stage in the life of the Church. Few of us in the Western Church have had the authentic experience of poverty that he has had in his own lifetime to date. His personal detachment from worldly goods is an example and a challenge to all of us. He has a real love for the poor, the sick and the vulnerable. This has given him the authenticity to move the question of justice and the unacceptable gulf between rich and poor further up the international agenda.

The word 'mercy' has been constantly on Pope Francis' lips and he has designated the year 2016 as the 'Year of Mercy'. I notice another word has been used frequently in recent times – the word *patienza*, meaning patience. I had the joyful experience of concelebrating with him last year at his morning Mass. I thought that he looked very tired and no wonder. He had just returned from a very demanding visit to Cuba and the United States and was now participating in the Synod of Bishops. Already, a small but quite significant group of bishops had submitted a document to the Synod opposing any change to the traditional application of Church teaching. In a brief exchange of words with Pope Francis after Mass, I recalled that as a young priest Pope John XXIII constantly used the exhortation *Corragio*: to have courage in the midst of difficulties. Pope Francis' immediate reply was *corragio e patienza*. Perhaps I am reading too much into a brief exchange of words but I feel that Pope Francis is recognising that change in the Church is a slow process and those who feel that change/development/renewal is needed must have patience.

Where is Pope Francis leading us? I would like to think that he is leading us back to Christ. It will be a long road back for many of us. Some of us may feel tired and disillusioned and too old to care about a new direction for the Church. Some younger people may look to a Church for more certainty than Francis offers and may be unwilling to embrace the challenge that the journey of the heart will demand of us. To all of us – young and old – Pope Francis' example is a pointing to hope in the future of our Church. It is that hope that Christ has given us through his life, death and resurrection.

Pope Francis speaks of the joy of the gospel. So too these are joyful and liberating times. Somewhere along our journey of life we seem to have lessened our enthusiasm for, and love of, that gospel message. We may have given up our freedom to the enslavements of rules and regulations and, indeed, to a comfortable lifestyle and allowed Christ's radical message of mercy and love to be imprisoned in compromises, untruths and worldly attachments.

Now a man has come from 'almost the ends of the earth' and is reminding us that Christ came to bring the Good News to the poor, to set captives free. It is my hope that, as we journey with him and with Christ, we may be freed from whatever captivity has taken hold of our lives.

10

My Experience of Church

A Church in control

I grew up in an Ireland where faith and practice were simply part of life. Few, if any, boundaries existed between citizenship and Catholicism, between faith and religion. Obedience to God and to our religious superiors – the priests and bishops – was a necessary ingredient for any kind of normal life. We went to Mass on Sundays in the local Camblin church, said the rosary every evening and participated in the variety of other religious activities of that time.

We were Catholics and Ireland was a Catholic country. We liked to think that Ireland was still the Island of Saints and Scholars with Irish priests and religious spreading the Catholic faith across the world. There was a certainty about our Catholicism that was justified by the absolute conviction that our Church was the one true church and was, therefore, entitled to exercise its power, not just in worship but in all areas of life, be it medicine or education, be it arts or literature, be it work or leisure. There was also power inextricably linked to that Catholicism stemming from an image of a God who would one day call us to account for all the wrong things that we did in life.

That was the Church into which I was ordained to the priesthood in 1959. It was a Church deeply conscious of its own rightness and, indeed, righteousness. Sunday Mass attendance was in excess of 90 per cent among Catholics. People went regularly to the sacraments of Confession and Communion and attended sodalities and missions in large numbers. All seemed to be well and there was little need for change. It was the era of the pyramidal Church, with the pope – the Vicar of Christ – at the apex. Underneath the pope were the bishops, then came priests and religious and at the base were the laity whose principal roles were to 'pray, pay and obey'. The priest welcomed you into the world through Baptism, nourished you with the Eucharist and saw you out of the world with Extreme Unction. 'To die without the priest' was the ultimate tragedy. Inevitably, this structure of Church gave a power beyond merit to priests and bishops and fashioned a Church which was rigid in its teaching and sometimes oppressive in its ministration.

I have no expertise in ecclesiastical history but I understand that this model of Church had its origins in the Council of Trent (1645–53), which sought to put order on both doctrine and discipline in a Church challenged by the Reformation. This model was reinforced by the definition of infallibility at the First Vatican Council. The model was further consolidated in Ireland in the second half of the nineteenth century by Cardinal Cullen of Dublin and like-minded Irish bishops. This same period saw a rapid growth in the foundation of religious orders and congregations, both male and female, which set up schools in almost every town in the country. Following Catholic Emancipation in 1829, the process of building churches in every parish continued throughout the nineteenth century. There was a significant increase in the number of priests being educated in the newly established Maynooth and in other ecclesiastical colleges throughout the country. The great missionary work of Irish priests and religious was already underway. By the time the twentieth century arrived, we had an Irish Church which, judged in the light of human standards, was extremely successful. With that success came power and control, and little desire for change.

That Church received the full backing and obeisance of the newly established independent government. It has been suggested – and with some justification – that the Church and the government established an 'unholy alliance' in which the Church and its various institutions took on the task of looking after those people who did not fit in with the ideals of morally correct citizenship. Over the past twenty years the serious injustice done to the people who were placed in these institutions has been revealed. But for decades the close partnership between Church and State continued and there was little demand for change.

Winds of change

By the late 1950s, however, there were stirrings of change coming from elsewhere. After almost twenty years in office Pope Pius XII died in October 1958 and was succeeded by John XXIII. At almost seventy-seven years old, it was hardly expected that Pope John would undertake any major change. The contrary proved to be the case. He summoned the Second Vatican Council and spoke of the need of *aggiornamento*: updating and adapting the work of the Church to the needs of the modern world. The Second Vatican Council embraced the spirit of change and renewal. For me and my fellow young priests, the Council allowed us to imagine new possibilities for the Church in Ireland, which was also experiencing that movement towards change.

Pope John's opening of the Second Vatican Council was a timely fit for this mood for change. It allowed us to imagine new possibilities. Two of the most outstanding documents of the Council proved to be the *Dogmatic Constitution on the Church* and the *Pastoral Constitution on the Church in the Modern World*. The former, known by its Latin title *Lumen Gentium*, emphasised that the Church was to be understood less in terms of bishops, priests and religious and more in terms of all the People of God whose calling is to be at the service of humanity. The *Pastoral Constitution on the Church in the Modern World*, known as *Gaudium et Spes*, outlined the pastoral implication of that Church understood as the People of God. The opening paragraph of *Guadium et Spes*, headed 'Solidarity of the Church with the Whole Human Family', set the tone:

The joy and hope, the grief and anguish of the people of our time, especially those who are poor or afflicted in any way, are the joy and hope, the grief and anguish of the followers of Christ as well. Nothing that is genuinely human fails to find an echo in their hearts. For theirs is a community of people united in Christ and guided by the Holy Spirit in their pilgrimage journey towards the Father's Kingdom, bearers of a message of salvation for all humanity. That is why Christians cherish a feeling of deep solidarity with the human race and its history (n. 1).

One hears the echo of this in the opening paragraphs of Pope Francis' *Evangelii Gaudium* and in his entire vision of Church today.

The Irish bishops returning from Rome after Vatican II varied in their enthusiasm for change. Archbishop McQuaid of Dublin assured the people that they need not worry, that their faith would not be disturbed. In fairness to the same archbishop, he put in place a number of initiatives inspired by the Council in the years following. Among these, perhaps the one which made the strongest impact was that of sending a small number of talented priests to the United States to train in broadcast media, especially television. This gave birth to the *Radharc* team, which produced high-quality television programmes on a variety of religious related subjects in the following twenty years. The initiative also sowed the seeds of the Catholic Communications Centre, which did valuable work in training priests, religious and some laity in media work and communications generally.

The Council gave new impetus to further education of priests and laity. At the time, the more recently appointed staff in Maynooth played a significant role in extending courses in theology throughout the country. These initiatives were followed up in some dioceses through continued adult catechesis courses over the following thirty years.

There were significant changes in the liturgy with the vernacular replacing Latin. Churches were reordered and adapted to facilitate the newer understanding of liturgical worship. The old understanding of the priest saying Mass with his back to a silently praying people was replaced by the concept of priest and people sharing in the celebration.

The Bishops' Conference set up a variety of commissions and agencies promoting and supporting new pastoral initiatives. One of the most fruitful of these was the setting up of Trócaire in the early 1970s. Trócaire is the Irish Catholic agency for overseas development which continues today to initiate and promote social and economic activity in some of the most deprived parts of the world.

It was an exciting time to be a priest with many new activities breathing new life into the Church. Being involved in the setting up of the Catholic Marriage Advisory Council (Accord) in our own diocese in the late 1960s gave me an enriching experience of working very closely with married people and young couples preparing for marriage.

Looking back some fifty years later, we take for granted all of these pastoral activities that followed the Council and gave hope that a new model of Church was emerging. But all was not change. Since the writings of Malthus early in the nineteenth century, the question of the world's capacity to support an ever-increasing population was being discussed. This was given new impetus in the middle of the twentieth century with the advances in medicine for fertility control. Gradually, people began to call into question the Catholic Church's position on family planning. Some people had hoped that the Council might have addressed the Church's teaching on family planning and some bishops felt the need to address the issue at the Council.

However, Pope Paul intervened and suggested that he would appoint a commission to study the matter. This papal commission had just one married couple there as a married couple. There were only two other married couples on the commission, but they were also serving in their professional capacities. There were also doctors, scientists of various disciplines and priest theologians on the commission. After lengthy deliberations, and by a significant majority, the commission recommended in its report to Paul VI that, at least in some circumstances, artificial contraceptives should be morally acceptable. Even though there was one agreed report of the commission, with a very small number of dissenting voices, those who dissented wrote a separate report, which had no standing with regard to the papal commission, and submitted it to Paul VI. It recommended that there should be no change in the traditional teaching. This has since become known as the 'minority report' but this is a misnomer, as it did not issue from the papal commission as constituted by Paul VI. It was generally expected that the Pope would accept the majority recommendation of the commission. After a long and, we believe, agonising consideration Pope Paul issued the encyclical entitled *Humanae Vitae* which reaffirmed the traditional teaching of the Church on sexuality and family planning.

The reaction to the encyclical was very controversial. For some it was the only possible decision the Pope could make. A change in such teaching was unthinkable. For many who had hoped for, and indeed anticipated, change it was deeply disappointing. Not obeying teaching of the Church in moral matters is as old as the Church itself, but this was something different. Here there was actual dissent from, or at least questioning of, the teaching itself. Very many theologians and priests, and even some bishops, either questioned the teaching or tried to interpret it in a manner that would lessen its impact. There was much discussion on the role of conscience. As for the people on whom it had most impact, namely childbearing couples, the vast majority simply ignored it. They felt it placed an unbearable burden on their relationship. I believe that the questioning of, and dissent from, the teaching of *Humanae Vitae* was a watershed in the Catholic Church.

The 1970s continued the opening up of Ireland to the wider world. Many factors were contributing to this opening. In particular, these come to mind:

- Free secondary education initiated by Minister Donogh O'Malley in 1967 was now contributing to a more educated public and was opening the possibility of third level study for increasing numbers of young people.

- After some years of preparatory work, Ireland joined the European Economic Community on the 1 January 1973. This increased our awareness of belonging to the European Community and indeed began to considerably benefit the Irish economy.

- Irish Television was coming of age. In particular, Gay Byrne's *Late Late Show* began discussions on topics that had previously been seen as within the domain of the Church; topics such as marriage, priesthood, religious life and indeed subjects that had almost been taboo for public discussion up to now, such as sexuality, family planning and sexual orientation. It was not that the show did not allow presentation of the Church's point of view on these issues; we were happy to have very worthwhile contributions to these discussions from people like Frs Fergal O'Connor, Eamonn Casey, Peter McVerry, Sister Stanislaus Kennedy, Joe Dunne and many others. What was new was that it was now acceptable to challenge the Church's position on different issues and to criticise the sometimes authoritarian positions of individual bishops.

Yes, times were changing. While a survey of church attendance in 1972 indicated that 73 per cent of Catholics went to church at least once a week, there was a gradual decrease in younger people attending church. We consoled ourselves by saying that they would come back when they got married and had children and there was no need to worry – our churches were still pretty full and there was an ever-increasing lay participation in Church activity. The laity was gradually becoming involved in parish councils, school boards of management, finance committees, ministries of the Word and the Eucharist. Towards the end of the decade (1979) we had the visit of the young, vigorous and charismatic Pope John Paul II, which certainly added to the feel-good factor and reassured us that all was still well.

Church and State
There were, however, other conflicts developing. Since the foundation of the State, the Catholic Church had worked very closely with successive governments. This relationship was enshrined in the 1937 Constitution, which recognised the 'special position' of the Catholic Church. The reality was that while the special position had no legal status, it did illustrate the close ties between Church and State. These close ties were seriously tested in 1955 when the Minister for Health Dr Noel Browne's Mother and Child Scheme was deemed by the bishops to be contrary to Catholic social teaching. The clash resulted in Dr Browne's resignation because his cabinet colleagues felt that he should have accepted the bishops' advice and amended the bill to their wishes. While the bishops won the battle many would have felt they lost the war. The issue resulted in a lot of bitterness and recrimination.

It was seen by many as another example of bishops using a heavy hand against anyone who did not accept their directives. Again, in the 1960s there were some tensions between bishops and the government on the issue of amalgamation of primary schools. This matter received much attention after Bishop Michael Browne challenged George Colley, the Minister for Education, at a public meeting in Galway. Further media attention followed when a young TCD student, Brian Trevaskis, called the Bishop of Galway a 'moron' on *The Late Late Show*, because of what he perceived as the extravagance and cost of the new Galway Cathedral when there was still so much poverty in the country. While the educational issue would remain on the agenda for some years ahead, perhaps the more significant factor was that it was becoming clear that bishops could no longer be exempt from public challenge or criticism.

During the 1970s the law banning the importation and sale of contraceptives received much attention from legislators and bishops. There was growing consensus among the legislators that the law needed to be changed, but there was a reluctance on the part of the government to deal with the matter, lest they incur the wrath of the bishops, and indeed, of a significant number of the Catholic population. The issue was highlighted in 1971 when members of the Women's Liberation Movement took a train to Belfast, bought contraceptives and returned to Dublin, publicly displaying their purchases, and no action was taken against them. Several attempts were made during the 1970s to change the law. Eventually, the law was challenged in the courts when contraceptives, ordered from abroad, were seized by customs. The challenge was successful on appeal to the Supreme Court. This decision put pressure on the government to introduce legislation permitting the importation and sale of contraceptives in 1974. To the surprise of all, the proposed bill was defeated because the Taoiseach, Liam Cosgrave, and six of his colleagues voted against it. The existing law remained in place, therefore, until 1979 when the Minister for Health, Charles Haughey, introduced a bill permitting the sale of contraceptives in limited circumstances. The act stated that contraceptives were only available on prescription from a doctor, who had to be satisfied that they were being used for *bona fide* family planning purposes. This was largely interpreted at the time as meaning only married couples could access contraception.

The Minister's own description of the bill as 'an Irish solution to an Irish problem' found its way into discourse in Ireland as a phrase describing a timid and ambivalent attempt to solve a problem. The issue of contraceptives remained on the agenda in the years following, until the law was further amended in 1992 to make it much less restrictive.

Northern conflict

The very serious violence in Northern Ireland began in 1969 and continued to escalate in the early 1970s. Gradually, an increasing number of politicians were beginning to understand the fears of the Unionists in relation to the Republic's attempts to interfere in Northern affairs. Garret Fitzgerald, who became Minister for Foreign Affairs in 1973, was particularly passionate in trying to allay these fears. As he saw it, there were several issues that gave the Unionists reasonable grounds for regarding the Republic as a sectarian state dominated by the Roman Catholic Church. There had been, until its removal by Jack Lynch's government in 1972, the 'special position' of the Catholic Church enshrined in the Constitution. Also in the Constitution was the ban on divorce. There was the strict application by the Church of the *Ne Temere* decree. This decree attempted to ensure that all children of a marriage between a Protestant and Catholic be raised in the Catholic faith. The effect of this decree was that the Protestant population in the south of Ireland was shrinking rapidly. As early as 1973, as Minister for Foreign Affairs, Garret Fitzgerald raised the issue of *Ne Temere* with his counterpart at the Vatican, Cardinal Casseroli. In his autobiography, *Just Garret*, he states that he found the Cardinal evasive on the issue. Casseroli suggested that he should speak to the Nuncio, to Cardinal Conway and some other bishops. The bishops' response was that Rome would not allow any such change.

A few years later, in 1977, Fitzgerald met with Cardinal Benelli, who was effectively Prime Minister of the Vatican, about the issue. Benelli suggested that he should speak with Pope Paul VI in relation to the whole question of Northern Ireland. At the meeting with the Pope, Fitzgerald explained that there was an appalling situation in Northern Ireland to which they were trying to respond in a positive and Christian way. He suggested a less strict application of the *Ne Temere* decree would be helpful in allaying the fears of the Unionists and contribute to the work for peace. He was very disappointed with the Pope's response – 'somewhat shell-shocked', in his own words. The Pope, while recognising the tragic situation, said that this could not be a reason to change any of the laws that kept Ireland a Catholic State. Garret suspected that the Pope had been briefed that he was a dangerous liberal, bent on destroying Catholicism in Ireland – someone who had to be admonished in no uncertain terms and whose expressed concerns about the Northern Ireland tragedy should not be taken seriously.

There was a further deterioration in the relationship between the government and the Holy See some years later. The government had taken a strong position on the hunger strike in Northern Ireland. The Holy See, presumably pressured by some Church sources in Ireland including the Nuncio, Gaetano Alibrandi, attempted to undermine the government's stance. The Taoiseach, Liam Cosgrave, reacted strongly. He was not prepared to take lessons from anyone on how to deal with the IRA and instructed his minister to respond accordingly to the Vatican.

The tension between the government led by Garret Fitzgerald as Taoiseach and the Irish bishops continued in the 1980s. In 1986, the government held a referendum proposing to abolish the constitutional ban on divorce. The position taken by the Bishops' Conference was that, while upholding the teaching of the Church on marriage being a lifelong commitment and therefore indissoluble, they would not tell people how they should vote. However, some individual bishops made it clear how they felt people should vote and many priests used the pulpit to oppose the lifting of the ban. The proposed constitutional change was defeated by a significant 63 per cent majority. The constitutional ban on divorce was finally removed in 1995 by a small majority of 51 per cent.

Ongoing tensions
In the midst of all of these controversies the majority of people were continuing to attend church regularly. Parents continued to bring their children for Baptism, schools

continued to prepare children for First Communion and Confirmation, couples continued to opt for church as a venue for their marriages and almost all sought Christian burial. At the same time, however, the number of those departing from regular practice continued to increase, especially amongst the younger people. The traditional teaching of the Church, especially in the area of sexuality and marriage, was simply being ignored by them. Also, there was a very rapid decrease in the number of young people offering themselves for priesthood or religious life.

While an increasing number of lay people were becoming involved in a widening range of Church ministries, they were mainly from an older age group. Vatican II, despite the best efforts of many priests, seemed to be fading into the background. If anything, with the passing years there appeared to be a rowing back of Vatican II, or at least a belief among certain members of the Church leadership that a lot of our difficulties as Church were caused by misinterpretation of the Council documents. Some people in the Vatican itself were clearly attempting to resist any attempt at change. There were efforts to reintroduce the Latin Mass. There was the instruction issued by the Congregation for Divine Worship, *Liturgiam Authenticam*, which insisted that new translations into vernacular used in the liturgy must be as close as possible to the original Latin. This resulted in giving us an English version of the Mass which is far removed from what we would regard as Standard English. There was swift action against any priest or bishop who asked for serious discussion on issues such as compulsory celibacy, the role of women in the Church, the exclusion of people in non-sacramental marriage unions from reception of the Eucharist and the teaching on family planning. Efforts, especially by female religious, to adapt their work to new areas of life were frowned upon. Pope John Paul II on his visits to South America made clear his distrust of some aspects of Liberation Theology with its strong emphasis on social and political activity in support of the poor.

Nothing, however, prepared us for what was to happen in the 1990s when a whole series of scandals broke over us in tsunami-like fashion. I have dealt with this issue elsewhere in this book. There can be little doubt that the issue of clerical child sexual abuse led to increasing numbers of people turning away from the Church and church attendance. During a period after the various official reports, I received regular letters in the post from people who wanted to formally declare their disaffiliation from Church. I found it a moving experience, especially when among those wishing to disaffiliate were some of my own friends. These were but a tiny fraction of those who decided to unofficially disaffiliate from the Church. The departures were not confined to young people. Many who had been very loyal to Church decided to opt out. However, I respect their decision and I see them as people who retain a sense of their own spirituality.

I believe there were several other contributing factors to people's disillusionment with the Church, apart from the various scandals. Over the years, many Catholics were unhappy about what they perceived as an oppressive role the Church played in their own lives and in society.

As I write in early 2015, we have just been through another referendum in which the Church and State have again been on opposing sides. The constitutional amendment that 'marriage may be contracted in accordance with the law by two persons without distinction as to their sex' was passed by a significant majority of 62 per cent. What was particularly striking about this referendum was that so many young people, unattached to any political party, played a major role in the 'yes' campaign. Again, it showed that our Church's understanding of sexuality and sexual mores has little meaning for our younger generation.

In all of these battles between Church and State – Noel Browne's Mother and Child Scheme, the two constitutional referendums on divorce and the Marriage Equality Referendum, the legislation in regard to contraceptives and the application of the *Ne Temere* decree on marriage – the Church has been presented as restrictive of human freedom and lacking in compassion. We have found it hard to accept the reality that State law is not obliged to reflect the teaching of any particular church.

I am often saddened that practically all our disagreements between Church and State appear to be around areas of sexuality. I wish our controversies were more about justice – about care for the poor and child poverty, about health care and homelessness, about the increasing gap between rich and poor at home and across the world.

In conclusion, where are we as a Church right now? We are certainly far removed from the Church into which I was ordained in 1959. We are a Church that has lost the loyalty and trust of so many of our people. It is clear that the vast majority of our young people do not see the Church as relevant to their lives. Our parishes are served by an ageing clergy who will not be replaced when they pass on. I have a sense too that many of us older clergy have become tired and disheartened and that we settle for simply continuing to provide what we regard as the essential services. And yet I believe that the Spirit of God is with us and leading us toward a more relevant model of Church. It will be a long journey.

I have no idea how the Church in Ireland will be twenty years from now. But if given a choice between the certain, powerful and controlling Church in which I was ordained and the wounded, humbled and, I believe, more honest Church of today, I would have no difficulty in making my choice.

11

A Journey Through Illness

An emergency

There was an extraordinary sense of peace and calm as I looked out across a perfectly manicured playing pitch. There was no sound, no players and no spectators. Was it Croke Park, Aviva or Semple Stadium? It didn't occur to me to ask which it was as I was in a state of euphoria. The euphoria did not last, though. I was gradually regaining consciousness. I heard the familiar voice of my niece at the end of the bed but when I tried to respond I found I could make no sound. I began to realise that there was a large tube down my throat, another smaller one in my nose, some drips feeding into veins and a catheter. The familiar voice whispered that the operation was successful. I drifted in and out of consciousness.

Slowly, I began to recall that on the previous evening, 22 November 2013, when at home a feeling of discomfort had developed quickly into an unbearable pain. I made contact with the local medical centre and was driven there by two friends whom I had called. There followed a midnight rush by ambulance to Limerick Regional Hospital. I still remember being told by the paramedic that we were entering the tunnel under the River Shannon. I felt that I would probably get there alive as we were now only minutes away from our destination. As the trolley on which I lay was wheeled in, it was met by a small team of medical people, some of whom had obviously been summoned from their homes. I heard the word 'aneurysm' as I underwent a scan. I answered a number of questions, including who is next of kin, and I signed the necessary consent form.

I am told that the lifesaving surgery lasted more than six hours. It was successful but I was warned that the days following would be difficult. They were more than difficult. I felt shattered, not just physically but also mentally, emotionally and spiritually. My initial reaction was to wrap myself up in a shell of self-pity and disconnect myself from the world around me with no thought for anything except my own discomfort. Healing began very slowly. Milestones such as sleeping for a couple of continuous hours, being able to shave, take a few tentative steps, were counted by the day. I was told that six to twelve months was the estimated recovery period.

Some dark days

Released from hospital after seven days, I was transferred to Cahercalla Community Hospital in my home town of Ennis. While it was something of a homecoming to a place where I had often ministered as a priest, the shattered feelings did not disappear. In fact, they became more acute in the weeks that followed. I felt totally broken, both emotionally and spiritually, and I now had plenty of time to reflect on my condition. The reality that I had been so close to death became a frightening thought. At times I asked myself would death have been an easier option. Such thoughts led to the dreaded question: did I really believe in life after death? The night prayer from childhood again became very meaningful and relevant:

Now I lay me down to sleep
I pray the Lord my soul to keep
And if I die before I wake
I pray the Lord my soul to take

'I am afraid to live and afraid to die,' I confessed to a close friend who visited me. I had lived my life in a world of faith for close on eighty years. It was not that I always took that faith for granted or that I hadn't struggled at times between belief and serious doubt. Still, I could honestly say that belief in God gave meaning and purpose to my life. And yet at the very time when I had come so close to death, there appeared to be so little there to reassure me. I still remember struggling at times with 'I offer my suffering with the sufferings of Christ'. The sentiment which I had sometimes preached to others did not come easily to me.

The eternal question of pain and suffering become more acute by the day. While indulging in my own self-pity, I began to become more aware that so many others had far heavier burdens to carry than I had – the family two rooms away keeping vigil night and day with a young mother journeying through terminal cancer, my own friend and priest colleague battling with Parkinson's for more than thirty years, a close friend trying to cope with the recent reality of widowhood, another with sudden total loss of sight. The daily news bulletins at the time carried harrowing reports of the two million refugees and their children from the Syrian conflict struggling for survival.

I think I reached my lowest point while listening to the *Documentary on One* on RTÉ Radio, on a dark Friday evening. (The documentary was produced by Ciaran Cassidy and narrated by Joe Duffy.) The programme traced the horrendous suffering of the family of Thomas Niedermayer. Thomas was a native of Germany but lived with his family in Belfast where he was manager of the Grundig factory. He was kidnapped – apparently with a view to payment of a ransom – and was murdered in 1973. His body was found some years later in a rubbish dump. His wife and two teenage daughters, who actually witnessed the kidnapping, later returned to Germany. During the following twenty years, in separate incidents, all three took their own lives, leaving just two teenage grandchildren now living in Australia. The story just tore me apart. Tears flowed while I listened. Whether they were tears of self-pity or pity for those whose lives had been so cruelly destroyed I don't know – probably a mixture of both. It was a story of the futility and destructiveness of violence in the name of a so-called noble cause.

I was reading two books at this time – one was Pope Francis' inspirational letter in which he speaks of 'The Joy of the Gospel' which 'fills the hearts and lives of all who have encountered Jesus'. He invited us to 'a renewed personal encounter with Jesus Christ or at least openness to letting him encounter them'. At the same time, I was reading *The Empires of the Indus* by Alice Albinia. The Indus is the great river which flows two thousand miles through Tibet, India and Pakistan. The author traces the history of the river and its surrounding people through ten thousand years. For me, however, at the time it was just another story of violence against, and suffering of, innocent people in the thousands of years before the birth of Christ. Somehow, I could not reconcile the message of joy, peace and love given to us by Pope Francis with the violence, pain and suffering of the people of the Indus valleys. The eternal question remained: where was God in the midst of all this pain and suffering? Indeed, I also found myself asking where was my faith in that God of love; a faith I had preached so easily in times past. My reading was painfully mirroring the actual struggle for recovery in my own life there and then.

During those dark days, I found myself physically pacing the hospital chapel several times a day repeating the only words I could find – 'Jesus, Jesus, Jesus.' There were no flashes of new light, no inspirational experiences. Gradually, over time the darkness began to lift. I began to get a sense of peace that somehow I could continue to trust in the Lord and that he would accept that trust. It wasn't that all my questions were answered, but rather that I could live with some uncertainty and be happy to let the Lord take care of it all.

Again, after some more time passed I was able to attend the Eucharist on a daily basis and this restored something of my own sense of priesthood and added to that sense of peace. For some months afterwards, I continued to attend Mass rather than celebrating at the altar as chief celebrant. While I have, of course, often attended Mass as a member of the congregation, it is a new experience to sit in the pew each day over a long period. I found it an enriching experience to concentrate on the prayers of the Mass without having to attend to any liturgical norms. Pope Francis speaks regularly about encountering Christ. I'm sure he sees this encounter with Christ as something which is, or ought to be, a permanent feature of our lives. I found that attending the Eucharist gave me some sense of that encounter.

Looking back, I have a sense too that one of the things that sustained me during those dark days was the assurance of being loved by a small number of close friends and loving them in return. While deeply appreciative of the messages of goodwill from many other people and their supportive prayers, I believe that at such a time one also needs the loving and more immediate support of one's closest friends. We men and, maybe more, we celibate clergy are often slow about expressing or even mentioning our love for each other. We still have much to learn in this regard, especially from our female friends. Hopefully, even at this late stage of life, I can learn to be less reticent about my appreciation of such loving support.

During my recovery period, healing continued at a slow pace. I had to learn to be patient and to accept that the world goes on quite normally without any input from me. Recovery from serious illness requires one's full attention. Perhaps the biggest challenge is how to cope with the time that can no longer be filled with the busyness of life. Ever since, I have found myself naturally giving much thought to the question of life and death, about the fragility and preciousness of life and the reality that death comes to all of us. I had been in what appeared to be vigorous health and within a matter of hours I was very close to death. It wasn't just about the fragility of the body, it was about the fragility of the whole person – body, mind and spirit. It was about the fragility of life itself. The experience has, I hope, taught me something of the wonder, the mystery and the sacredness of life and of its preciousness.

A time for reflection

One is reminded, too, of the reality that death is never far away. I believe that most of us when in good health think of death as something far away, if we think about it at all. This appears to be true even for those of us who are in our later years. We probably know people in their nineties who are still in good health, so why shouldn't we live to a ripe old age? I now realise that good health into your nineties is certainly not the norm and that at eighty-one death is not just inevitable but probably, at most, only a few short years away. It is not that I feel I have to live the remaining years waiting in fear. In fact, I am hoping that I will be able to enjoy the remaining years with a greater sense of gratitude to the Lord for the gift of life itself. None of us is without some fears in relation to death. None of us knows, or can grasp, what life after death is going to be like. That very uncertainty can raise all sorts of doubts so the faith struggle continues. I still cling to the belief that our God – and all people's God – is a loving, forgiving and compassionate God. Perhaps what I fear more than death itself is what might happen before death – poor quality of life, prolonged illness, loneliness, etc. For the moment, I am satisfied to leave it all in the hands of that loving God.

I have been reflecting, too, on how our Church sees the link between our suffering and the suffering of Christ. Over the years of priesthood, I often preached on that theme but I found it quite difficult to apply it to myself when my turn came. That year, 2014, I read with added interest the message of Pope Francis for World Day of the Sick:

The Church recognises in you, the sick, a special presence of the suffering of Christ. At the side of – and even within – our suffering is the suffering of Christ; he bears its burden with us and reveals its meaning. When the Son of God mounted the cross he destroyed the solitude of suffering and illuminated its darkness. We thus find ourselves before the mystery of God's love for us which gives us hope and courage.

I do, of course, assent to this teaching and it has much more meaning for me at this distance. Yet, I found it very hard to apply it to my own case in those darker days.

I have had over the years some sense of gratitude in relation to life. I felt that the Lord had been kind to me and that I had been lucky in regard to family, education, friendship and loving relationships, in regard to priesthood itself and the various ministries to which I had been appointed. It is not that I haven't done my share of complaining, but I always felt that life had been very kind to me. In particular, in recent years I was very conscious of the blessing of good health and would often have thanked the Lord for that blessing.

Since my illness, I sometimes wonder how generous my prayer of thanks was. Was there something of the Pharisee's prayer, 'Thank God I am not like the rest of men'? I have minded my health. I gave up smoking twenty-five years ago. I take regular exercise and am disciplined in my eating habits. I feel I was even a little boastful in telling people about my good health and how pleasant retirement was proving to be. Somehow various illnesses happened to other people and I didn't consider myself as a candidate for that fate. So, perhaps, I need to look again at my prayer of thanksgiving for good health. Albert Nolan in his book *Jesus Today* has a challenging chapter headed 'With a Grateful Heart'. He speaks of prayers of thanksgiving and suggests that such prayers can become selfish if I simply thank God for all the blessings he has given me, without any sense of gratitude for the blessings he has bestowed on others. A truly grateful heart, he reminds us, will thank God for everything that is good in my own life and in the lives of others.

Nolan also makes the point that to nourish and develop a grateful heart we need not just the occasional prayer of thanks for some special blessing that comes our way. Prayers of thanks should be regularly on our lips. Hopefully, in the future my prayers of thanksgiving will be more generous by including giving thanks for all God's blessings.

Over the years as a priest I would have been a fairly regular visitor to hospitals and have found hospital staff generally welcoming and caring. As a patient, however, I directly experienced their extraordinary generous care. Starting with those at our local medical centre, through ambulance paramedics, the team who did the surgery, the staff of ICU and general ward, I had a sense of being surrounded by people who really cared about me and wanted to do all in their power to enable me to get better. That experience was repeated every day for the following six weeks in the local Cahercalla Community Hospital where I was convalescing. I am grateful to all of them and to the priests and staff at the local presbytery who cared for me for a few months after my leaving hospital and before I returned to my own home where the journey into illness had first begun.

I believe that it is very important that our society should really value and respect those who generously care for the sick, the poor and the vulnerable. That valuing and respecting is not just about how we pay them – a norm too often used in our society. Their generosity and kindness goes far beyond monetary consideration.

For most of my life I enjoyed good health and the recent experience of personal illness came as a shock to me. It has also been a humbling experience. It taught me at once that I was no longer fully in charge of my own life. I was very much dependant on the professional skills and care of others. It increased my awareness of how important the support of family and loved ones is. I have learned that any false sense of my own importance is very unwise. I hope, too, that I have a deeper sense that my life, like everyone else's life, is very much in the hands of the Lord.

Enriching experience

I would like to think that the experience, painful though it was, has been an enriching one. I believe it has forced me to reflect more deeply on my own struggles with faith. While that reflection has not yielded comforting certainties to the difficulties I may have, I feel I am much happier now to accept a degree of uncertainty and to continue to place my trust in a loving God. Indeed, much of what follows in the remaining chapters of this book has been inspired by this deeper reflection about life and death, faith and hope, what it means to be human and to understand something of the sacredness of that humanity.

Again, I think the experience will make me more aware of and sensitive to the suffering of others. I am not suggesting that I was unaware of the suffering of others up to now but the direct experience of serious illness does help to identify more closely with that suffering. Again, I am satisfied that the bonds that bind me to those that I love and who have been so kind to me in a dark period of life have been strengthened.

I hope that these feelings will persist now that I have made a full recovery. I recognise, of course, that I could easily revert to where I was before the illness, but I feel that the experience has been deep enough to have some lasting effect. At this stage, I have one principal hope for whatever years are left to me. Fr Brian Grogan, in his book *A Spirituality of Ageing*, put words on his own hopes in this regard, saying he would like to be 'a loving presence in the world around me'. Presuming his kind permission, I would like to make his words my own.

Now as I write in October 2015 I can report that I have made a full recovery – at least this is what I have been able to say each day for the past few months. I feel that I have made the journey through illness and arrived at a point of full recovery, thank God. I see each day as a blessing – one more day to be lived and enjoyed. While one never knows what tomorrow may bring, I believe that I now have a greater sense of well-being than I have ever experienced for years past. I try to live each day as a blessing from God. I have no illusion that life is going to be perfect from here onwards, but it is good right now and for that I am grateful. As to my being 'a loving presence' for those around me, I am still working on that!

12

Faith

The God question

'I believe in God.' This opening phrase of the Apostles' Creed is the most fundamental statement we can make in relation to our faith. All other statements of what we believe depend on it and flow from it. Belief in God gives a particular meaning and direction to our lives. It affects our view of the world and its purpose. It influences how we see ourselves and others and how we relate to each other. It has profound implications for how we feel we ought to live and how we hope to die.

It is hardly surprising then that since the very beginning humankind has been preoccupied by the 'God Question'. It is hardly surprising that it continues to occupy the minds and hearts of people in today's world. There can be little doubt that in the Western world an increasing number of people struggle with faith and many believe, or at least suspect, that God is an illusion. Witness the extraordinary interest in Richard Dawkins' *The God Delusion*, published in 2006. There may not be many who are as certain as Dawkins that God is an illusion or delusion, but I have a sense that more and more people are questioning. Dawkins and other scientists tell us that it all began with a 'big bang' and that over the millions of years it evolved from inanimate to animate, from animate to plant, to animal, to man/woman and for the unbeliever it all ends with a hole in the ground, returning whence we came.

In Ireland today, many of our young people regard faith and religious practice as quite irrelevant to their lives. It is not that they are convinced unbelievers; it is more that they do not see faith or practice as relevant to their lives. Many of them have departed our churches in recent years, giving the scandals of sexual abuse as their reason for doing so. While the scandal of abuse is an understandable reason for their departure, I believe that, for many, the reason lies deeper in the weakening of faith.

This weakening of, or struggle with, faith is not confined to the young. I have a sense that many of our older people are also struggling with faith. As parents and grandparents, they have been loyal to their faith and practice and have encouraged their children to do likewise. These children, now mature adults living good, decent and caring lives, no longer see the point in attending church or indeed in any expression of faith. I paraphrase how one parent put it to me:

> We have practised our faith all our lives and encouraged our children to do likewise. Now our adult children live decent honest lives but faith and practice seem to have no meaning for them. And at this stage I am no longer sure what I believe myself. I have no questions about the values preached and lived by Jesus Christ – the values of truth and justice, compassion and love. But I am not sure about Christ being God. I am not even sure about belief in God. Could it all end with the grave?

Is this man unusual in his thoughts? I think not, and the more I talk with people the more I am satisfied that very many of his age group are struggling with faith. There is, I believe, something of a crisis of faith in Ireland and that crisis is not just confined to the young.

And where do you or I stand in regard to faith?

We are, of course, dealing with the unknowable in that God is beyond the limits of human understanding. Yet questions like the following constantly surface:

- Where did we come from?

- Where are we going?

- Is there something more than a big bang?

- Is there something more than chance or random selection?

- Is there something more at the end of life than a hole in the ground?

- Is there a deeper and more profound meaning and purpose to life?

In the beginning

Perhaps we should begin at the beginning. What is your story of faith? What is my story of faith? My story, like most stories, began in childhood. Among my earliest memories is that of being tucked into bed at night by my mother and being led by her in the prayer:

Now I lay me down to sleep
And I pray the Lord my soul to keep.
And if I die before I wake
I pray the Lord my soul to take.

Today she would probably be challenged with 'don't be frightening the child'. Yes, I think it did make me a little afraid at times, especially the 'if I die before I wake' bit, but for the most part I rattled it off without much thought. It became as much a kind of soothing mantra as a real prayer. Nevertheless, I believe that this and similar prayer experiences were part of the early foundations of faith and belief in God which have greatly shaped my life.

Like so many of my generation, I grew up in a family and surrounding community in which belief in God was an accepted and unquestioned fact. My parents were people of faith. My mother was very pious in the traditional sense. Every crisis or lesser difficulty was treated with a whispered 'Sacred heart of Jesus, I place all my trust in thee'. I wouldn't use the word 'pious' of my dad. He was a man who simply believed in God and lived his life in the shadow of that belief. His faith was a practised, but unspoken one.

A very Catholic home

The atmosphere in the home was a strongly religious one. The rosary was recited each evening after tea. We went to Mass every Sunday in the local Camblin church. Monthly Confession, Communion, sodalities, novenas, together with annual trips to Lough Derg, were simply part of life. There was no more need or inclination to ask why these things were done than to ask why we saved hay in the month of June. Words like faith, belief and religion were not part of the day-to-day conversations. We were Catholics and that said it all.

Not everyone in our community was Catholic. We had several Protestant families in our neighbourhood and fine, decent neighbours they were. But, as far as the rest of us were concerned, they were wrong and why they couldn't see they were wrong was somewhat puzzling to me! It was fine to work side by side with them saving hay, threshing corn or picking potatoes. It would be very wrong, however, to pray with them or to enter their churches. Indeed, I can still recall a very strong disagreement between my mum and dad on this very issue.

In 1944, Bob Lewis, a Protestant neighbour died and my dad indicated that he would be going to Bob's funeral. My mum warned him that he was not to go inside the gate and should not listen to whatever prayers they said. Dad insisted that Bob Lewis was a good, decent neighbour and that he was going to the funeral whether or not it was against the rules of our Church. He went to the funeral and went to confession the following Saturday night. The priest told him that he would have to get special dispensation from the bishop to forgive my father because participation in a Protestant funeral was a reserved sin. Dad returned to the priest some weeks later and received absolution. My mum was pleased but I am not a bit sure about my dad's contrition! It was some years later that I heard what I believe was the reason for my dad's insistence on attending Bob's funeral. Back in 1925 when my dad and some neighbours were planning to buy a large farm and to divide it up between them, they heard that Bob Lewis was also interested in buying it. There was some intimidation used to prevent him from doing so. What part my dad played in that intimidation I don't know, but I believe that he respected Bob all the more because he had not let those events prevent them becoming good neighbours and friends.

Early images

The image of God that was being formed in me was that of an elderly gentleman with a beard, up there in the sky. It wasn't that anybody told me he was elderly, but he had been around for a long time, so he must be elderly! Besides, the people who spoke to me about God, about being good, about Holy God wanting me to be good were all elderly people – all adults are elderly to a child. So God himself must be old and religion itself was old.

And the elderly gentleman could be cross with you if you did something bad. He was someone to be feared. And that fear grew stronger when we began to hear about hell and purgatory. He was up there seeing everything that was happening down here and he kept a list of all the bad things we did. This list would be produced on judgement day to decide whether it was hell or, at best, purgatory. At times, it was a rather frightening prospect. It is difficult to know how much this image of a fearsome God derived from home or from primary school. It is true, however, that the early beliefs learned at home were affirmed and supported in the primary school.

That simple, unquestioning faith persisted through adolescence and my teenage years. In a secondary boarding school largely run by priests, faith and religious practice were taken for granted. Belief in God was supported by Sheehan's *Apologetics*, which set out the five proofs of the existence of God; proofs originally set out by St Thomas Aquinas. God was the 'Unmoved Mover', the 'Uncaused Cause', etc. Faith was also supported by the teaching of history. The English had invaded our country, kept us in subjugation and persecuted us because of our faith. Catholicism and nationalism went hand-in-hand and we sang 'Faith of Our Fathers' with gusto before hurling matches. God continued to be a God to be feared, a God who punished sin and rewarded goodness.

I can't claim that these teenage years were very traumatic. There were not the pressures, either academic or social, from which teenagers today suffer. There was no such thing as social media which appears to be such a significant influence in the lives of young people today. There were, of course, the normal teenage pressures of seeking independence, of becoming a person in one's right and the anxieties of what the future might hold. There was, however, the quite significant pressure of coming to terms with one's sexuality in an environment in which there was virtually no discussion on the issue except for the strong emphasis on the virtue of chastity. The fear of God's punishment certainly loomed large in this area.

Looking back at a distance of sixty or seventy years, one is amazed at the simplicity of it all. God was in heaven, the pope was in Rome, Catholics were right and Protestants were wrong, and the archbishop of Cashel threw the ball in at All-Ireland Finals! It is not that I regret that simplicity or certainty. It was a faith that satisfied the Ireland of the time and the people who led us on that early journey.

God: The Mystery

In June 1952 I sat my Leaving Certificate and in September of the same year I began studying for the priesthood. I have often been asked why I made that decision and what my motivation was. I suspect that my motivation was complex in that many different factors contributed to the decision, but I have no doubt that fear of God was a significant one. I would have felt that being a priest would give me the best chance to save my soul. I like to think that over the years of studying for priesthood my motivation for being a priest became more generous – that it was more about serving people rather than saving my own soul. The image of a God to be feared was gradually evolving into a God who is compassionate, forgiving and loving.

It was never an easy transition from the God of fear to the God of compassion and love. As the years of priesthood moved along, there were certainly times of real struggle for faith and belief. I never had any difficulty with the values preached and lived by Jesus Christ – values of justice and peace, of compassion, forgiveness and love – even if I didn't always practise them. But I did struggle, and still do at times, with the belief that Jesus was divine and with the whole concept of God.

When we speak of God we are, of course, reaching out to the unreal – unreal in the sense that God is beyond our rational experience. We cannot see God, we cannot touch God and we cannot hear God. God is 'Mystery', not just a mystery among mysteries; God is 'The Mystery'. And if God is beyond our ordinary human experience, if God is 'Mystery', then it is hardly surprising that some people will conclude that God is an illusion, or that many more will find belief something of a struggle. And I think the struggle to believe is part of many of us, as people of faith. Think of the times when we wonder where God is in a world of war and tragedy, in a world of hatred and violence. And where is God in a world of pain and suffering within families? And I don't know any family who hasn't experienced pain and suffering. Where is God in a world where some of us have much more than we need while millions are constantly on the brink of starvation?

At a personal level, and as Church, we are challenged by the pain and suffering in our world and we often feel helpless in the face of it. We respond in various ways: some will be angry, some will be sad, some will judge and blame others, and some of us will choose not to dwell on the question in order to protect the already fragile state of our own lives. Some will come to believe that there is no God. How could a God, whom we claim to be good and loving, allow such pain and suffering? There is no simple answer to this question, and those who use it to argue that there is no God rarely claim that they have an answer either. The only way that they can live is to strive to create a world where there is less evil, less pain and suffering. That, too, ought to be the first response of those of us who claim to believe in God. Faith and belief do not give us any simple answers to the questions of evil, pain and suffering. Maybe it is because of these wars and tragedies, the hatred and violence, the evil, pain and suffering that we need God and that we need to come together in prayer and worship. Do we come together in prayer and worship because we believe or is it that coming together in prayer and worship helps us to believe? I am more comfortable with the latter – that coming together in prayer and worship helps and supports my belief. Belief is not sustained by prayer and worship alone. It needs to be nourished by our efforts to try to live our lives following the example and teaching of Jesus Christ.

Where is God?

The 'where is God' question brings to mind the terrible and yet inspiring story by Elie Wiesel, a survivor of the Holocaust, in his book entitled *Night*. He tells a very moving story about coming back from work one evening to the concentration camp and finding three gallows erected in the assembly ground. Three prisoners, two men and a boy, were selected for execution. As they stood on the platform with ropes around their necks, a man shouted 'Where is merciful God, where is he?' The chairs on which the three stood were pulled from beneath them and then there was silence. The prisoners were then marched past the gallows. As Wiesel reached the spot the two men were dead but the boy, being lighter, was still struggling between life and death. He says, 'Behind me, I heard the same man asking: "For God's sake, where is God?" and from within me, I heard a voice answer: "Where He is? This is where – hanging here from this gallows ..."' It is sometimes in moments of darkness and despair that God is nearest to us.

There are no simple answers to the problem of pain and suffering. Theologians and spiritual writers invite us to unite our sufferings with the sufferings of Jesus Christ and thus participate in the great mystery of salvation. While such an understanding may be in keeping with Church teaching, it presumes a depth of faith that is beyond many of us and will hardly resolve the doubts and questions which beset us at times. And perhaps these very doubts can challenge us to move out of the comfort zone which we sometimes build around ourselves. Garrison Keillor, the famous American writer and storyteller, writing about Holy Week in the *Chicago Tribune* in March 2008, said:

Holy Week is a good time to face the question: Do we really believe in that story (Passion, Death and Resurrection of Christ) or do we just like to hang around with nice people and listen to organ music? There are advantages, after all, to being in the neighbourhood of people who love their neighbours … Scepticism is a stimulant, not to be repressed. It is an antidote to smugness and the great glow of satisfaction one gains from being right … Jesus was rougher on these people than on the adulterers and prostitutes. So I will sit in the doubter's chair for a while and see what is to be learned back there.

I think it is no harm for any of us to sit in the doubter's chair occasionally. The late Cardinal Martini of Milan put it this way:

There is within each of us two people – one a believer, one a non-believer. They quarrel and fight with each other. Why not help people to discern between the two voices, not by giving space to the believer but to the non-believer?

Any attempt to divide people into believers and non-believers is much too simplistic. Belief and non-belief are rarely two well-defined opposing positions. There is a continuum from the totally convinced believer and the totally convinced non-believer and I suggest that the number of people at either end of that scale is quite small. The vast majority of us are somewhere in between the extremes and we move at least a little along that scale at different times in life. There is something of belief and non-belief in most of us.

Pope Benedict, in his meeting with religious leaders in Assisi in October 2011, spoke of the people in the growing world of agnosticism 'to whom the gift of faith has not been given, but who are nevertheless ... searching for God'. He suggests that they – the agnostics – are aware of the deficiencies of aggressive atheism but also feel let down by religious people whose lives do not point towards God:

> They take away from militant atheists the false certainty by which these who claim to know that there is no God and they invite them to leave polemics aside and to become seekers who do not give up hope in the existence of truth and in the possibility and necessity of living by it. But they also challenge the followers of religions not to consider God as their own property, as if he belonged to them, in such a way that they feel vindicated in using force against others.

I wonder could we say something similar about the partial agnosticism that dwells in the shadow side of many of us. I believe that the questions and doubts can help us to dialogue more honestly with the agnostic and those struggling with their faith. They challenge us to live out in our own lives the faith we profess. The questions and doubts help to prevent us from regarding God as a sort of possession which sets us apart from or indeed above those struggling to believe. It is well to remember that Christ died for all of us – believer and non-believer alike.

A variety of approaches
There are many ways we can approach the question of faith and belief. In the past some philosophers and theologians

argued that the existence of God could be established by reason alone. The advancement of science has given explanations to so many of the former mysteries of life, death and happenings in the natural world, that few would agree nowadays that reason alone can suffice. Faith and belief must respect and take account of reason because we can sometimes use faith and belief in a manner which totally defies reason. Pope John Paul II wrote a full encyclical on this subject of faith and reason. I understand him as saying that faith devoid of reason risks becoming superstition and blind prejudice: witness some of our Catholic practices of the past, such as the All Soul's Day practice of dashing in and out of a church with a quick prayer each time, believing that each visit released one soul from purgatory; witness the frightening belief of the 9/11 hijackers that they would receive a very pleasurable reward for their terrible destruction of atheistic Westerners. On the other hand, reason without faith risks self-absorption and detachment from reality. Our Western world of growing humanism, relying on reason alone, has created an expectation that a perfect order can be established here on earth. Atheistic communism, again relying on reason alone, was based on the expectation that another type of perfect order could be established. Neither approach has been particularly successful. It is not that humanism or commun-ism do not promote a worthwhile ideal; it is rather that reason alone without faith is incomplete. Humanism is lacking in that deeper meaning and purpose of life and risks reducing people to a living organism operated by the laws of chemistry and biology.

We can say that faith is a gift from God, and so it is. That gift is given to us through our parents and the believing community in which we grew up. Had I been born to non-believing parents or into a non-believing community, it is likely that I would be a non-believer. And if faith is a gift, it is not something that I can earn nor can it be forced on me. I can, however, reject it or simply allow it to be inactive and to die.

Faith is also an act of trust – trusting those around us and trusting our deepest instincts and longings. Some speak of this act of trust as something of a leap in the dark, in that faith is not always accompanied by the certainty and clarity that we experience in other areas of our lives. I would prefer to see faith as a leap out of darkness into light in the sense that faith is a light that enlightens and gives meaning and purpose to our lives. Pope Francis, in his very first encyclical entitled *Lumen Fidei*, speaks of the 'light of faith' lighting up the darkness and of the uncertainties of life without faith: 'The light of faith is unique since it is capable of illuminating *every aspect* of human existence' (n. 4). The encyclical continues to speak of the light of faith as born from an encounter with God and 'which penetrates the core of our human experience' (n. 32).

And so, faith is often presented as a personal relationship with God. A relationship expressed in prayer and worship, trusting that one is safe in his care. I notice in recent years that theologians increasingly emphasise this relational aspect of faith. They begin from the premise that we are created in the image and likeness of God. If I believe that I am created in the image and likeness of God, I must then in some way participate in the essence of God; the core of that essence being the relationship of love between three divine persons. Relationship has to be in some way at the core of my humanity. When studying philosophy, we described man as a rational animal. In this context that seems an impoverished description. I am not just an animal capable of reasoning; I also have the capacity for, and a need for, relationships. Each one of us has the need to relate to others and if we do not, or cannot, relate we become isolated and alone.

If we feel isolated and alone for a long period, we can become incapable of empathy and incapable of having a close, warm relationship with another person. The capacity for and the need of relationships is part of our nature, part of who we are.

Faith as relationship

The most fulfilling and enriching relationship we can have is a relationship of love. All of us, to be fully human, need to love and to be loved. All our experiences of love are in some way a participation in God's love. Recently, I spent some time with a couple who had had their first child only two months previously. The child was lying on his back on the floor. The father and mother were on their knees gazing lovingly at their child, smiling, touching and making baby-talk noises and watching for the child's reaction. At each reaction they exchanged loving glances with each other and then their attention was back on the child. I was deeply moved by the experience of seeing these three people in such an intense relationship of love. Reflecting on the experience, I found myself asking if there was a glimpse of the Trinity here. The Father loves the Son and the Holy Spirit is the personification of their love. Here the father and mother love each other and the child is the personification of their love. Yes, an image of the Trinity – a family created in the likeness of God. In my own experience, I find that at those times that I have a strong sense of loving and being loved, faith comes easier. On the other hand when I feel a heavy sense of loneliness or that nobody really cares, my faith seems much weaker. Speaking of God's love for us can hardly have much meaning for someone who has never had any real experience of love in his or her life.

At this late stage of my life I think that faith and belief in God is more and more a decision – that amidst the struggles and doubts and questions, amidst the pain and tragedies of life I have made a decision to believe. It is not just a reasoned, intellectual decision but a decision of mind and heart. Neither is it a private, individual decision between God and me, isolated from others and from my relationship with others. It is rather a decision that I am part of or want to be part of a believing community relating to each other and to God. A reasoned attempt to prove the existence of God may give us some assurance at an intellectual level. Trying to live out our faith in our daily lives is much more effective in deepening our faith than any such intellectual exercise. I have a sense of a God who has been generous and kind to me in my life and for that I am grateful. It is a decision that makes sense of my life and that without it life for me would be meaningless and without purpose.

I accept that there are millions of people out there who haven't been as lucky as I have been; people whose lives have been blighted by poverty and deprivation, by earthquakes and tsunamis, by abuse and lack of love.

We always rejoice at the birth of a child. The wonder, the joy, the innocence of new life gives us hope for our world. And yet this joy and this innocence will gradually be taken away in our competitive world and will finally have to yield to death. If all were to end in death it would be understandable that we might ask if it would have been better if this life had never been given, especially if it was a life blighted by ill health, by poverty, by violence and abuse. If there is no 'beyond', then to me life is meaningless. Belief challenges me to fight against such unfairness and injustice.

I have, therefore, in some way made a decision to believe, or a decision to confirm and continue the faith given to me in earlier years. It is not a blind faith, it does not rule out all doubts. It is a decision of mind and heart that belief in God makes sense of my life and of my relationship with others and without it life would be meaningless and without purpose.

13

Who Is Your God?

In the previous chapter I was reflecting on faith, on belief in God and indeed on the struggle that at times belief can be. I was reflecting on my own journey of faith. That journey took me from an early God of fear through struggles and doubts towards a God of forgiveness, compassion and love. I see faith not only as a gift from God but also something of a decision of the heart and mind based on the conviction that this faith gives meaning and direction to my life. Without that belief, life would appear to me to be without meaning and purpose. I would like to continue that reflection by asking:

• Who is the God in whom I believe?

• Who is the God in whom you believe?

• Who is your God?

• Who is my God?

Do the very questions 'who is your God', 'who is my God' invite the response 'God is God'? In a sense he is not my God or your God, he is the God of all of us, and yet all too often we fashion a God who fits into our own very prejudices, a God with whom we can live comfortably.

The kind of God in whom I believe is going to have a significant influence on the way I try to live my life. Different kinds of gods have been used throughout history to justify all sorts of behaviour. Angry gods have had to be placated, kinder gods have been beseeched for favours, generous gods have been thanked and unfair gods have even been cursed. God has been used to fight wars, with both sides believing that God was on their side. God's name has been invoked in support of crusades, inquisitions and burnings at the stake. The perpetrators of the horror of 9/11 were confident that God would reward them for their deeds. I suggest that we have sometimes used God as some sort of a super ATM in which we put in certain requests, accompanied by prayers, and expected our needs to be automatically delivered. I mentioned earlier All Souls Day, the day on which we raced in and out of churches believing that we released a soul from purgatory with each visit. Again, there was the expectation that attending Mass on nine successive First Fridays would guarantee salvation and other similar exercises that were supposed to deliver results automatically.

So, who is your God? Who is my God? I think of God as some Person, some spiritual Power who is responsible for the world and all that it contains, guiding and inviting us towards goodness, friendship and love. He is somebody who is a little removed from me and maybe that is where I want to keep him – not too close lest he make too many demands on me. I do believe that this God has given me life and that he cares for and loves me. Do I love God? I am not sure. I never feel the same way about God as I feel about a small number of people whom I love and who love me. I sometimes feel that we talk too easily about loving God as if it was the same as loving another person.

No more fear

What I can honestly say is that the fear of God which was there in my earlier years has largely disappeared. I cannot accept that a God who gave me life, a God whose constant message through Jesus Christ is a message of love would condemn me to eternal punishment. I find it difficult to believe that this loving God would condemn anybody to eternal punishment. I think I can understand those who profess to be atheists, but I find it very difficult to understand those who profess to be Christian and yet present us with a God who is harsh and judgemental. The only God in whom I can believe at this stage of my life is a loving, compassionate and forgiving God.

The question arises as to how we form our image of God. Naturally, our early image of God is going to be formed by our parents and the surrounding community. As we grow towards adulthood that image is developed and nourished through the study of scripture and through the experience of life. For us as Christians the most authentic source for our image of God is the Bible. The first part of the Bible, which we call the Old Testament, is really a history of the relationship between God and the people of Israel. The God presented there is the creator of the world and all that it contains. He is all-powerful and all-knowing. He has made a covenant with his people and protects them and helps them to defeat their enemies: 'I will be your God and you shall be my people' (Jer 30:22 NJB). There is little doubt that this image of God as formed by the people of Israel before the

coming of Christ is often a harsh God. Presumably they
formed their image of God from what they saw of the powerful people in their society – the kings, the court prophets and
the high priests. These were people of power and, sadly, were
often tyrannical and cruel. Thus their image of God was often
associated with anger, with harshness and punishment. He
was a God whom you offended at your peril:

> The Lord Almighty says that disaster is coming on one
> nation after another … on that day the bodies whom the
> Lord has killed will be scattered from one end of the
> earth to another … They will cry out in distress because
> the Lord in his anger has destroyed your nation and left
> your country in ruins (Jer 25:32 GNB).

> The Lord will roar from heaven,
> And thunder from the heights of heaven.
> He will roar against his people,
> He will shout like a man treading grapes
> (Jer 25:30 ff. GNB).

It would be a misreading of the Old Testament, however,
to suggest that the image of God is exclusively the all-
powerful, harsh and to-be-feared God. On balance there is
more emphasis on love than on fear, on mercy than on
harshness, on kindness than on severity. The psalms,
especially, constantly give praise to God for his goodness,
forgiveness, compassion and love.

Psalm 136 gives thanks to the Lord for his enduring love
and Psalm 50 speaks of God's mercy, compassion and
forgiveness. God is presented in Psalm 26 as a God not to be
feared, but as a God of support:

The Lord is my light and my salvation,
Whom shall I fear?
The Lord is the stronghold of my life,
Before whom shall I be afraid? (Ps 27 NRSV)

Again, God is presented as the one who cares for the poor and those who are suffering. In the Old Testament there is the recurring theme of the Israelites breaking faith with their God but, again and again, being invited back by him and being forgiven.

When we come to the New Testament we are in a new phase of our relationship with God. The opening passage of the letter to the Hebrews speaks of this new phase:

In the past, God spoke to our ancestors many times and in many ways, through the prophets, but in these last days he has spoken to us through his Son. He is the one through whom God created the universe, the one whom God has chosen to possess all things at the end. He reflects the brightness of God's glory and is the exact likeness of God's own being (Heb 1:1–3 GNB).

Here we are faced with the mystery of the Incarnation. The mystery of God becoming man in the person of Jesus Christ: 'He reflects the brightness of God's glory and is the exact likeness of God's own being.' Jesus is the revelation of God, God showing himself to us in human form. Jesus came to reveal the Father to us. He was God in human form. He is Emmanuel, meaning God is with us.

Philip said to him 'Lord show us the Father: that is all we need.' Jesus said:

Whoever has seen me has seen the Father (Jn 14:9 GNB).

It is through the life and teaching of Jesus Christ that we can form our image of God. That image is of a God who above all else is compassionate, forgiving and loving.

Our God is a forgiving God
The Father's willingness to forgive is a constant theme in the life and teaching of Jesus. The parable of the Prodigal Son presents the son who demands his share of the inheritance. He leaves the family home, squanders his fortune on 'wine, women and song' and finds himself homeless and hungry. He returns home to ask to be taken on as a servant but his father is having none of that and welcomes him back as a beloved son (cf. Lk 15:11–32). The message surely is that no matter what evil I have done, no matter how selfishly I have behaved, no matter how unchristian I have been, God – the prodigal father – is always ready to forgive once I turn to him and ask for forgiveness.

Several other passages in the gospel have the same theme of forgiveness. The woman caught in the act of adultery is asked, 'Has no one condemned you?' She replies, 'No one, Lord.' And Jesus said, 'Neither do I condemn you, go, and do not sin again' (Jn 8:11 NRSV). There is the parable of the lost sheep and the joy of the shepherd in finding the lost one (cf. Lk 15:4–7).

On the cross Jesus prays, 'Father, forgive them, they know not what they do' (Lk 23:34 GNB). God's willingness to forgive is a constant; it is always available whenever I ask. There are no limits placed on it: 'not seven times but seventy times seven' (Mt 18:21–23 GNB). Our God is a forgiving God.

The mystery of new life

With family: my sisters Kitty and Maura and my brothers Eddie and John

In the grounds of Bishop's House, Ennis

Viewing repair work on Ennis Cathedral spire

Millennium Committee at Bishop's House, Ennis

The Pilgrimage of Reconciliation, December 1999

The Pilgrimage of Reconciliation

The Pilgrimage of Reconciliation

Putting the finishing touches to the building project in South Africa

With Sr Ethel Normoyle and Seamus Ryan at a building project in South Africa

With Sr Ethel Normoyle in Capetown, South Africa

With Pope Francis, 2015

St Flannan's centenary celebrations, 1982. Michael O'Kennedy,
Taoiseach Garret Fitzgerald, Sabina and Michael D. Higgins

Our God is a compassionate God

Compassion is a constant theme in the life and teaching of Jesus Christ. In the gospel he invites us to 'be compassionate as your Father is compassionate' (Lk 6:36–38 NJB). Compassion is that quality of 'suffering with', of 'feeling for' people who are in pain. Compassion involves not only a sharing in the pain of others but also in the joy of others. Jesus didn't lecture people about their moral duties. He simply saw their pain and trouble and tried to bring healing to them. He reached out in a special way to the sick, the poor and those who were deemed to be sinners. He is regularly moved to compassion at the pain of others:

Come to me all you who labour and are overburdened and I will refresh you (Mt 11:28 NJB).

When he saw the crowds, he had compassion for them, because they were harassed and helpless, like sheep without a shepherd (Mk 6:34 NRSV).

Some other New Testament passages such as Lk 7:13; 10:30–35 and Jn 11:35 are further examples of God's compassion. Jesus' death on the cross was the ultimate act of compassion. Our God is a compassionate God.

Our God is a loving God

Many of us were reared with the idea that God would love me if I were good. I had to earn God's love. That idea of God's love is very understandable; that is how we behave in our relationships with others. We love those who love us. We love or at least like those who are kind to us, who respect and affirm us. Our love is conditional on the behaviour of others

towards us. It is hard to believe that God loves us uncondi-
tionally, that he loves me in a way that no one else loves me.
He loves me even if I do not return that love. The nearest we
get to unconditional love in humans is the love of a parent for
their child. A father or mother will continue to love their
child, even if the child rejects their love. Their love is not
normally conditional on the child returning that love.

I am created by God out of love and am held in existence
out of love. I am special in God's eyes, and not only me but
every person, no matter who they are or what they have
done, is special in God's eyes. I believe that the realisation
that each one of us is special in God's eyes and is loved by
God is more important than any dogma or moral code. And
if God loves me he surely wants me to be happy, to be free,
and to be alive. Jesus reminds us, 'I came that you may have
life and have it to the full' (Jn 10:10 GNB).

In the Old Testament, while God tends to be seen as the
supreme authority figure, he is also seen as having those
qualities of tenderness, mercy and love. In the New
Testament, Jesus presents God as a loving father:

> Think of the love that the Father has lavished on us by
> letting us be called God's children, and that is what we
> are (1 Jn 3:1 NJB).

Jesus not only speaks of God as his Abba/Father but invites
the disciples to use the word 'Abba' of God, thus drawing us
into a close intimate relationship with God. That intimate
loving relationship with our Abba should be seen as parental
– embracing father and mother. There are several references
in the Old Testament to God as mother:

Can a woman forget her suckling child, that she should have no compassion on the son of her womb. Even those may forget you, yet I will not forget you (Isa 49:15 NRSV).

I understand that the Hebrew word *rachamim*, meaning 'compassion', comes from the root word *rechem*, which means womb, and is used to describe God's mercy and compassion, again suggesting the intimate tenderness of a loving mother. (cf. *Jesus of Nazareth*, Pope Benedict XVI, p. 135).

Again and again, the scriptures speak of God's love for us (especially in 1 Jn 3:1–4 and 1 Jn 4:9–11 NRSV). The message of love is clear and simple and profoundly reassuring:

God is love, and whoever lives in love lives in union with God and God lives in union with him ... We love because God first loves us (1 Jn 4:16–19 GNB).

Jesus' own life was surely the very living out of God's love for us. In particular his address to his disciples at the last supper in chapters 15 to 17 of John's Gospel is a very moving presentation of his love.

Discipleship
It is comforting to believe that our God is a forgiving, compassionate and loving God. It is challenging to be forgiving, compassionate and loving in our own lives. But, as Christians, that is what we are called to be. We are called to be followers or disciples of Jesus Christ: 'Jesus ... saw a tax collector named Matthew sitting in his office. He said to him "Follow me". Matthew got up and followed him' (Mt 9:9 GNB). He called four fishermen Peter, Andrew, James and

John and 'They left their nets and followed Jesus' (Lk 5:11 GNB).

I personally prefer the term 'disciple' to 'follower'. I think disciple implies a lot more than mere imitative following. It is about putting oneself in the footprints of Jesus, living by his example and honouring his teaching. However, I am happy to see great merit in the idea of follower too as it implies that Jesus is always in our sight guiding us like a lighthouse might guide a ship at sea. We follow the light wherever it leads us.

My primary identity as a Christian is that of follower of Jesus Christ. That is my identity – who and what I am. Being a Catholic, Protestant or Baptist is secondary. The early followers of Jesus were called disciples of Christ. The name or title 'Christian' came later: 'It was at Antioch that the believers were first called Christians' (Acts 11:26 GNB). We are firstly followers of Christ, not followers of the Church. The Church is a community of followers – people who follow Christ. The Church helps us to follow Christ, but the Church is not an end in itself; it is rather a means to facilitate the continuation of Christ's mission on earth. I think that was what Pope Francis was saying when he talked about a 'self-referent' church, 'which keeps Jesus Christ within herself and does not allow him to go out' (Cardinal Bergoglio's talk to cardinals before the conclave).

This discipleship, this call to follow Christ is not always easy. Jesus reminded us that discipleship will at times involve suffering: 'Whoever does not carry his own cross and come after me cannot be my disciple' (Lk 14:27 GNB) and 'If anyone wants to come with me, he must forget himself, carry his cross, and follow me' (Mt 16:24 GNB). All of us would prefer if discipleship did not involve the suffering part. Pope Francis in his first homily to the cardinals stressed the centrality of following or journeying with Christ on the cross:

> We can journey as much as we want, we can build many things but if we do not confess Jesus Christ the thing does not work. When we journey without the cross and when we confess Christ without the cross, we are worldly, we are bishops, priests, cardinals, popes but not disciples of the Lord.

The suffering involved in following Christ can take a thousand different forms, ranging from the ultimate losing of one's life in martyrdom, through the very significant suffering in ill health of a loved one to the minor inconveniences of everyday life. Some spiritual writers invite us to offer our sufferings with the sufferings of Christ, thus participating in the work of redemption. I have often spoken on the theme of uniting one's suffering with the sufferings of Jesus. I have to admit that when I found myself in real suffering I found it hard to live out that teaching.

While discipleship does involve suffering, it is important to remind ourselves that Jesus' message is 'good news' and that our lives as Christians should surely reflect something of the joy of that 'good news': good news of the Incarnation, God entering our world in the person of Jesus Christ; good news of God's love for us; good news of our love for each other; good news that 'I came in order that you might have life – life in all its fullness (Jn 10:10 GNB)'.

Sadly our Catholicism is often perceived as forbidding us to do things we might like to do, as being oppressive and joyless. Is my discipleship good news? Is it a source of hope and joy or is it a burden?

We are disciples of Jesus Christ, journeying with Christ. We may be a long way short of the destination of fully living the values of Christ, but the journey, the following, is what we are called to. We are invited to try to live by the values which characterised the life of Christ – values of forgiveness, compassion and humility. Above all and encompassing all other values is the value of love.

14

Prayer

Prayer as communication

Central to any healthy relationship is good communication. If a relationship is to survive, grow and flourish, there needs to be good communication between the people involved. If our relationship with God is to survive, grow and flourish there has to be good communication between us.

I understand prayer to be a form of communication between God and us: private prayer being a form of communication between God and the individual person; public prayer between God and the praying community. Obviously, the relationship between God and us is very different from the relationship between us humans:

- Human relationships depend significantly on the human senses of hearing, seeing, smelling, tasting and touching.

- Human–divine relationships may involve some feelings but they do not depend entirely on the senses.

- Human relationships are like to like in that both participants are of the same nature.

- Human–divine relationships involve significantly different natures.

- Human relationships are not always relationships between equals (parent–child; teacher–pupil) but the inequality in human–divine relationships is of a totally different degree.

These significant differences mean that the form of communication between God and us is going to be quite different from the form of communication we have between each other as people. Nonetheless, there appears to be some similarities between the two. Several things come to mind when we think of good communication between people, especially if the relationship is one of love:

- Fairly regular awareness of and thinking about the other.

- Being concerned for the happiness of the other.

- Being open and honest with the other.

- Trusting the other.

- Sharing significant time with the other.

- Having a sense of gratitude towards the other.

- Being comfortable in the silent presence of the other.

I suggest that many of these characteristics of good communication between people will also be present in our communication with God in prayer.

A healthy prayer life will involve a fairly constant awareness of God in our daily lives – that God is never far from our mind. This awareness will involve an acceptance that we owe our lives, our gifts and talents to God. I do believe that for some people that constant awareness of God's presence is so much part of their lives that they are continuously at prayer. Brian Grogan in his book *To Grow in Love* quotes an elderly Jesuit as saying, 'I am either praying all the time or not praying at all.' I suspect while he may not be 'saying prayers', he is praying all the time through a constant awareness of God.

Openness and honesty are essential to good communication; otherwise trust breaks down. Openness and honesty are essential to a healthy prayer life. I don't suggest that any of us would attempt to be dishonest in our prayer, but I feel that sometimes we try to present ourselves to God as we think we should be rather than as we are. God knows us as we are and loves us as we are. His love does not depend on our being good. Openness and honesty involve recognition of our own goodness and our weakness. They involves acknowledgement of our successes and failures, joys and sorrows, hope and despair, faith and doubt. Is it, perhaps, in the times of failure, despair and brokenness that we pray best, clinging to the hope that God always desires our good.

Good communication will involve a sense of gratitude towards the other. When applied to prayer life it will involve a recognition of and gratitude for all our blessings. For the vast majority of us, our blessings far outweigh our difficulties – the blessings of life itself, of food and shelter, of friendship and love. We have indeed much for which to be grateful to God. In saying this, I am conscious that many people carry very heavy burdens in life – the burdens of ill health, the death of a husband or wife, the tragic death of a child, the caring for a child with special needs, the loss of a job. I have no idea of how I would cope with such challenges. I hope that placing our brokenness and even our anger in the hands of God might help to some degree to ease our pain.

Good communication involves spending time with each other. While in our prayer life there should be a fairly constant awareness of God, I believe that most of us need to set aside specific times when we try to give our full attention to God in prayer. For some this may take the form of short periods of prayer at different times during the day. For others it may be a longer period of prayer at one specific time. Others may choose to take part in prayer with the community at daily worship, such as celebration of the Eucharist. If we don't give time specifically for prayer we can easily drift away from any awareness of God in our lives.

All of us will have experienced the capacity of people who are in love to be comfortable to be together in silence. I believe that that capacity to be silent in the presence of God is an important aspect of prayer. We live in a noisy world. We appear to be uncomfortable with silence. Even when we go for a quiet walk many of us need to be plugged in to music. Do we feel uncomfortable in the presence of a silent God? Do we fear that God might be prompting us to change some area of our lives? I see the growth of the modern practice of 'mindfulness' as a response to that need for silence in our lives. (While mindfulness might be considered new, this practice of self-awareness has a venerable history in Buddhism.) The capacity to be 'still in the presence of the Lord' applies not only to private prayer but also to public prayer. I often think that we as priests are nervous about silence in celebrating liturgies. We can speak for ten minutes in a homily and still get quite uncomfortable with a minute's silence at the end of it. I'm not sure if it is my own discomfort or that I feel that the people become restless. It is easier to go straight into 'I believe in one God'. Again a short period of silence after Communion would be appropriate, but I think we feel that the congregation would like us to 'get on with it'.

Every prayer life is different and each one of us as we go through life has to try to discern what approach to prayer suits us best. It is not that one day we will find the form of prayer that will suit us for the rest of our lives. I believe that for most of us our prayer patterns simply evolve continuously throughout our lives. At this late stage of life, I find these habits emerging:

- I'm not good anymore at formal prayer, though I still normally recite the Divine Office each day.

- I often find it easier to pray in the company of others rather than to pray alone, though we are never more human than when we pray alone. There is no room for pretence when we pray alone.

- I am trying to develop the habit of just sitting in silence with occasional repetition of a short phrase such as 'Jesus have mercy' or be still in the presence of the Lord.

- I find my prayer more about reflecting on things, and more about giving thanks to God rather than asking for favours.

- I usually need a spiritual book or a piece of scripture to help me at prayer – read a bit, reflect on it and let it lead to prayer. I suppose it is my own version of *Lectio Divina*.

For those who are unfamiliar with *Lectio Divina*, it is a form of prayer which developed in the early years of monasticism and has had a significant revival in recent years. It can be used by a group of people or on one's own. Essentially, it is reading a piece of scripture, reflecting on how this reading might apply to my or to our lives at this time and allowing prayer to develop from it.

Pope Francis in his book entitled *The Church of Mercy* speaks of allowing the Lord to look at us. In addressing catechists he invites them to be close to Christ. He suggests that it is not enough for them just to have the title of catechists, but that in order to be effective catechists they must be close to Christ and to achieve that they must allow the Lord to look upon them: 'Do I find time to remain in his presence, in silence, to be looked upon by him? Do I let his fire warm our hearts?' He says that it is only by being close to Christ that they are then 'compelled in the love of Christ to go out to others bringing the message of Christ with them and to have the courage to go to the margins with this message'. Surely if we say this to catechists then we must say it to ourselves as priests, because we also are catechists.

Private and public prayer

Many of us tend to think of prayer as something very personal and, of course, prayer *is* very personal, but it also has an essential communal aspect. The view of prayer being purely personal and private fits in very easily with the current approach of our Western world, with its emphasis on individualism and in its widely held view that religion is a private matter, with no place in the secular world. The reality is that prayer is both personal and communal. It is personal in that it is an expression of my own relationship with God. It is communal in that we are not on our own in relation to God. We also relate to God as a community. This double aspect of prayer is reflected in the fact that our Church has traditionally promoted both aspects. All our liturgies are forms of communal prayer. At the same time, the Church has also recommended that we pray in the privacy of our own hearts but in that privacy we should have a place for others, especially those in need.

This double aspect of prayer has a solid foundation in the gospels. Jesus often withdrew from his disciples and spent time on his own in prayer. 'In the morning long before dawn, he got up and left the house and went off to a lonely place and prayed there' (Mk 1:35 NJB). 'He would go away to lonely places where he prayed' (Lk 5:16 GNB). He obviously at times felt the need to be alone to communicate with God. We live in a busy, noisy world and we need that stillness to be alone with God. Jesus also prayed with others. 'He took Peter, James and John with Him and went up a mountain to pray' (Lk 9:28 NJB). It is significant that there was that double aspect of the personal and communal in his prayer life. Perhaps the most heartfelt prayer of Jesus was his prayer in Gethsemane. He took with him Peter, James and John and asked them to keep watch with him. But then he moved on a little further, threw himself on the ground and prayed: 'My father, if it is possible take this cup of suffering from me! Yet not what I want but what you want ... Father, if this cup of suffering cannot be taken away unless I drink it, your will be done' (Mt 26:37–44 GNB). Here, Jesus prays alone and his prayer is focused on himself and his foreboding of what lay ahead of him.

The only recorded prayer that Jesus taught us is a communal prayer. It is addressed to 'Our Father'. We pray that God's name may be honoured and that his kingdom may be established. We pray that he may give us our daily bread, that he may forgive us and help us through temptation. The emphasis here is not on my needs but on our needs. It is natural and perfectly legitimate that I should reflect and pray in relation to my own needs. But in a healthy prayer life the emphasis will be on the needs of the community. The prayer attributed to St Francis of Assisi illustrates this focusing of communal needs:

> Lord, make me an instrument of thy peace,
> Where there is hatred, let me sow love;
> Where there is injury, pardon;
> Where this is doubt, faith;
> Where there is despair, hope;
> Where there is darkness, light
> Where there is sadness, joy.

Transforming our lives

Prayer, of course, is never an end in itself. It is a means rather than an end; a means of communicating with God, of drawing close to God and to Jesus Christ. If prayer is authentic, then it must have an effect on how we live our lives. It is not about feeling good after prayer, as we sometimes do. It is not about receiving favours for ourselves from God; it is rather about getting closer to Jesus Christ. It is about helping us to be more Christ-like by trying to transform ourselves to being better people by reflecting on our lives and seeing how we might be more compassionate, more forgiving and more loving.

Does it work? Does prayer help to transform our lives? It would be unwise to operate only in that expectation. There are times in all our lives when prayers seem either impossible or without any effect. Many of the great prayer-saints, such as John of the Cross, Teresa of Avila and Mother Teresa of Calcutta, have experienced such emptiness in prayer that they were tempted to abandon prayer altogether. I think most of us would feel that it would be presumptuous of us to attribute 'the dark night of the soul' to ourselves. There is little doubt, however, that we go through periods of dark night which require a trust that in itself is almost despairing that any help is possible, that the Lord knows best and will see us through the dark night into new light.

The question remains: does prayer transform our lives? It is always difficult to measure spiritual transformation, but I truly believe there is sufficient evidence to say that people of real prayer have become more Christ-like in their lives. It is hard to believe that reflecting on, and praying about, the teaching and example of Jesus Christ would not change our lives for the better.

15

Christian Hope

Angry young men

Though I enjoyed all of my twenty-five years teaching at post-primary level, I have no hesitation in saying that the most challenging, inspiring and hope-filled years were those of the second half of the 1960s. I fondly recall it as the era of the 'angry young men'. It was the time of student revolution when 'angry young men' in Ireland and across Europe – remember the Paris student riots? – were impatient to change the world. I belonged to a group of slightly angry young priests who were impatient to change the Church. We were nourished by the documents of Vatican II while other young men fed on Mao's 'little red book' (*Quotations from Chairman Mao Tsetung*).

There is no doubt that the 1960s was a time of great hope. Pope John XXIII had summoned the Vatican Council, John F. Kennedy became the first Catholic president of the United States, and the Civil Rights movement was spreading across the United States and was beginning to march in Northern Ireland. Freedom was in the air.

Somehow, as the years went by the angry young men became silent – too busy perhaps with marriages and mortgages, with family and finance. Their successor students seemed more interested in points than in peace, in jobs than in justice. The impatient young priests became parish priests, too busy perhaps with maintenance rather than with renewal. Vatican II seemed to have lost its urgency. Violence and war, poverty and injustice continued unabated. Pete Seeger's 'Where Have All the Flowers Gone?' was sung plaintively, with new meaning across the world: 'Oh, when will they ever learn?'

This is not to say that considerable progress had not been made in the intervening years. There were extraordinary advances in science, and technology, in medicine and psychiatry, in food production and education. There has been progress too in our Church. There has been greater involvement of laity in the daily life of parishes through parish councils, finance committees and a variety of new ministries.

The fight against poverty originally led mainly by Church-inspired organisations such as Concern and Trócaire has been significant. There has been a welcome move away from an oppressive theology which was more concerned with sin and damnation than with compassion, forgiveness and love. There has been, however, until more recent times a continued reluctance to allow real discussion on different issues in relation to sexuality and marriage, the role of women and indeed the role of laity in regard to any serious decision-making in the Church.

Like the students, we as Church appeared to gradually grow silent until we were suddenly awoken by the loud cries of scandal in the 1990s. Those of us in positions of responsibility found ourselves very poorly prepared to respond adequately to the revelations of child sexual abuse.

A variety of reports, shocking in the extreme, gradually sapped our morale. I have the impression that many of us priests and bishops became discouraged by the pressure of it all.

Holding onto hope

As an eighty-year-old I find it hard to rekindle the high hopes which obsessed us in those earlier years. There is still no end in sight to wars and violence, to hunger and poverty, to the massive injustice in the manner in which many of us enjoy more than our fair share of the fruits of the earth, while half the people of the world are constantly on the brink of starvation. On the day I write, our media report that nearly a thousand poor people from North Africa and elsewhere have drowned in the Mediterranean. They had been packed into small fishing boats trying to gain entry into Europe. We in Europe have so far done little to try to respond to this scandalous human trafficking. Yet Pope Francis challenges us not to allow these evils to be excuses for diminishing our commitment and fervour. He warns us against sterile pessimism and 'a defeatism which turns us into querulous and disillusioned pessimists'.

> While painfully aware of our own frailties, we have to march on without giving in ... keeping in mind what the Lord said to St Paul 'My grace is sufficient for you, for my power is made perfect in weakness' (2 Cor 12:9). Christian triumph is always a cross, yet a cross which is at the same time a victorious banner ... Let us not allow ourselves to be robbed of hope (*Evangelii Gaudium*, nn. 84–87).

So where is this hope in the midst of all this pain and suffering? It was in such a mood that I recently took up a small book entitled *Hope* written by the late Cardinal Martini of Milan. It is not the easiest of reads, but it has helped me a bit in trying to clarify my own understanding of the issue. Hope is so central to our lives. We often say 'where there is life there is hope'. I prefer to turn it around and say 'where there is hope there is life'. We cannot live fully if we do not have hope. Hope keeps us alive. Hope inspires us to press ahead, despite the difficulties. Hope enables us to survive and overcome evil, violence, hatred or even natural disasters; hope challenges us to live life and to live it in the fullest possible way. I have the impression that in our Church we speak a great deal about faith and love, but somehow there is little enough space in between for hope. Michael Downey in his book *Hope Begins Where Hope Begins* puts it well:

Hope is the very heart and centre of the human being. There is simply nothing more central to the human life. But, strangely, we human beings who need hope more than anything else in life have written little about it. In a good deal of Christian theology hope seems like the proverbial 'middle child' sandwiched in between the affirmations about the priority of faith and the excellence of love. Hope is the very condition for the possibility of faith and the action of love. Hope is the capacity in each one of us that is open to God's truth and love. It is that quality in the human being that is open to possibility to new things happening.

Christian hope

Martini, in his book, insists there are two essential aspects to Christian hope. On the one hand, hope must always have the expectation that the promotion of peace, justice and love among all people is a reasonable goal and that Christians must do all they can to promote these values. On the other hand, Christian hope must also be founded on the belief that we are on a journey towards where all our dreams of peace, justice and love will be fulfilled, where there will be no more hope, there will only be love.

These two aspects of Christian hope are intertwined and not two separate phases of life – doing one's best in life here and hoping that we will be rewarded in life hereafter. We are already on the journey towards God. As believers we trust that God is working in us and through us here and now, that ultimately we will reach that goal which is God himself. The kingdom of God is not something which is confined to life after death. The kingdom of God is present among us now as he invites us to work for justice, peace and love. The gifts we have, the blessings we enjoy are truly gifts from God. They are signs of God's generosity and love as we journey together in solidarity with each other until all of us will be enveloped in God's love.

Martini argues that any attempt to build Christian hope on only one or other of these foundations is doomed to failure. Our Western world has largely attempted to build its hopes on one foundation – that of material things such as money, possessions, power and leisure. While these things may give us temporary satisfaction, they can never answer that deep hunger and hope that is in the human heart for a better world. No sooner have we acquired what we hoped for than we immediately are looking forward to more of the same or to some other object that will satisfy our perceived need – the next holiday, a better job, a new love. Instead of enjoying and appreciating what we have, we move on to our next need. Many people who have experience of working in the poorer parts of the world say that hope is more alive among the poor than among us. They appear to get more satisfaction and joy out of the simpler things in life; they have a far greater capacity to celebrate together and to share what they have. They appear to be able to enjoy the present good moment without a constant need to look forward to the hopefully better one.

Hope that is built only on the other foundation – that all will be right after death – is also quite inadequate. Simple acceptance that 'the poor you have always with you' or that 'your reward will be great in heaven' can be an excuse to avoid our obligation to work for justice and peace on earth. Indeed, in its extreme form, the promised great reward in heaven can be used to justify the most evil of crimes such as that of 9/11, or other all too common modern-day atrocities like suicide bombings. Such thinking does a grave injustice to the dignity of the human person and their right to live a fully human life here on earth.

Christians who build their hope only on the foundation of belief in the afterlife can at times give credence to those who claim that such belief distracts from the task of working for a better world here and now. Some forms of modern atheism argue that religion, of its very nature, discourages people from the task of working towards people's economic and social well-being. Marx summed up this thinking in his dictum: 'religion is the opium of the people.' The logical consequences of this theory are that when such people gain political control they often violently, or in a more subtle manner, attempt to destroy any form of religious belief and practice. Such thinking undermines the eternal destiny and the dignity of the human person and reduces them to mere tools of economic well-being. Christian belief and hope sets no limits on the value and dignity of each individual and invites each of us to work in solidarity with each other throughout our lives here and now and toward our eternal destiny. Hope in a life to come should never lessen the responsibility to work for a better world here and now but rather should deepen our motivation to fulfil it.

The idea that hope can be founded only on the belief that all will be put right in the hereafter flies in the face of the example and teaching of Jesus Christ, who healed the sick, showed special love for the poor, the broken-hearted and the outcasts. He reminded us that our future fitness for the kingdom of heaven would be judged on how we fed the hungry, clothed the naked, took care of the sick, welcomed the stranger and visited the prisoner (cf. Mt 25:32–36).

Real Christian hope acknowledges that 'we have not here a lasting city' and that as limited human beings we will never succeed in building a perfect world where justice, peace and love is possible for all. This hope, however, insists that we must always work towards that justice, peace and love which will only be fully achieved in the life beyond death.

Christian hope is ultimately founded on the belief that our world owes its very existence to God and that God is an integral part of our history as human beings from the very beginning. Part of that history has been our unfaithfulness to God and his continued faithfulness to us. Having sent various prophets to call us back to him, he eventually sent his own son in the person of Jesus Christ who, through his death and resurrection, overcame sin and death and gave us the hope that we too can overcome sin and death. We live in the ultimate hope that our God is leading us towards that fuller life where there will be no longer pain and suffering, no longer violence and war, no longer hatred and injustice, and there will no longer be hope – there will be only love.

Many of us, maybe even all of us, have at times in life experienced the pain of losing hope. There have been times in my own priesthood when I found it very difficult to keep my hopes really alive and life-giving.

I feel in a different place at this stage of life – more happy to leave things in the Lord's hands. Ultimately, everything is in his hands and surely he is as much present with us today as he ever was; he would no longer be God if he were not always faithful to us, even at those times when we are unfaithful to him. And even if I have no way of knowing what it will be like in life after death, I am still happy to leave it in his hands. In the earlier language of the Mass we prayed to God 'to protect us from all anxiety as we await in joyful hope for the coming of our Saviour Jesus Christ'. I can't say that I am always 'waiting in joyful hope', but I do believe that the joy of new life in God's love will be beyond any joy we have experienced in life.

Going back to Martini's dual aspect of hope, I think that the 'angry young men' and the impatient young priests of the sixties placed the burden of hope too heavily on our belief that all was possible in the here and now. While I always regret the passing of the angry young men and of the impatient young priests who were in a hurry to change the world, I can now accept that significant change comes slowly.

Hope fostering change?

Thankfully, not just some priests but a great number of lay women and men are becoming the raised voices in the Church today. I have no doubt that they are growing impatient with the leadership of the Church which is slow to countenance change. In the context of hope, one might ask what shoots of hope exist for those voices seeking change?

I don't have an answer to that question. Yet I feel that the Church must, at the very least, open itself to discussion and dialogue. This will come about when there is a fundamental change of heart in all of us. A Church that is remote and unyielding is a Church that overlooks the values of Christ such as mercy and forgiveness and turns its heart into stone. And yet I believe the Spirit of God is with us and leading us towards a more relevant model of Church. Certainly, the year 2015, just ended, has presented more challenges to which all Christians are invited to respond, if we are to remain relevant in the modern world. In particular, I have in mind the following:

- The issue of climate change.

- The mass immigration of people from poor and strife-torn countries to Europe.

- The terrorist attacks in Paris.

- The Year of Mercy proclaimed by Pope Francis.

There are hopeful signs that the issue of climate change is at least being taken seriously by our world leaders. It is the first global issue on which all countries have committed themselves to work together in solidarity to save us from self-destruction. Pope Francis in his letter *Laudato Si'* has spelled out the invitation to all Christians to join in this commitment.

The mass migration of people from poorer and war-torn countries towards Europe is again a huge challenge. The unspeakable suffering of so many people in search of a secure place to live is sending a strong message to our society that we cannot continue to enjoy the abundant fruits of the earth while leaving so many of our brothers and sisters under the threat of violence and starvation. All indications are that this migration will continue into the future and we, as Christians, are challenged to respond by working toward a more equitable world.

The recent attacks in Paris brought home to us, in the West, our vulnerability in the face of terrorism. It has also reminded us that belief in a God can sometimes be used to justify the most evil of crimes. As Christians we are invited to reach out in peace and love to our brothers and sisters of different faiths and of none. I believe that history has taught us something of the failure of military interventions in other jurisdictions, where they seldom contribute to peace and justice.

I truly believe that, in the face of all these challenges, Pope Francis' designation of this year as the Year of Mercy is timely and prophetic. The belief that our God is a merciful and compassionate God invites us to be merciful and compassionate towards each other. It invites us never to stand in judgement of each other. It invites us to recognise and affirm the goodness in each one of us. It invites us to be aware of the goodness within ourselves and that every person, even the terrorist, is our sister or brother.

I believe we are at a very special time in human history – a time of crisis, but also a time of Christian opportunity.

In my brief meeting with Pope Francis he spoke of courage and patience as being important. I don't offer those words as a placatory gesture to those who seek change but rather with awareness of the empowering qualities of courage and patience. I suggest that the heart of stone will not be moved by anger or the force of argument alone but by the love that courage and patience will foster in all of us when we reflect on those qualities. Courage and patience when actively applied will bear fruit – break down barriers, open the way to discussion and dialogue, soften hearts and effect change. I believe that the Church requires a change of heart that will only come about when the heart of stone is eroded by love. I believe that we are Christians only when we love and that love for me is best expressed by the kindness of Christ. All our efforts for change must never overlook the power of that love. As a person of hope, I know no other way.

16

Do This In Memory Of Me

Two experiences of Eucharist

A few years ago, I was privileged to spend two weeks in Mombasa, Kenya as part of a group of two hundred volunteers building a school for blind and partially sighted children. It was a privilege to be with these people, who worked all the daylight hours in intense heat to provide suitable accommodation for about 180 children, all with special needs.

On the first Saturday there I was asked by the foreman if I would give them 'a quick Mass' on Sunday morning, so that they could get back to work as quickly as possible. I joked that there is no such thing as a quick Mass in Africa – it's only in Ireland we do 'quick Masses'! On Sunday morning I celebrated the 'quick Mass' as requested and afterwards I played a little truancy. Rather than getting back to the painting job to which I had been assigned, I went to the local church a few minutes away to concelebrate with the local Irish priest and his African community. This Mass was a totally different experience. It was two and a half hours by the time we got back to the sacristy after Mass.

Our own 'quick Mass' in the midst of cement, sand and concrete mixers was quite meaningful in that it was very much grounded in and related to our work. It was a moving experience in its own right, but I couldn't stop thinking of the contrast between the two celebrations of the Eucharist. Ours was something we needed to fit in, whilst theirs was a more prolonged and unhurried joyful celebration of faith. It involved singing and dancing – not me, at my age – on the way in. We sang and danced during the Mass, we sang and danced on the way out. Someone didn't just 'do the first reading'. The two readers carried the lectionary head high in procession up the central aisle accompanied by a group of people involved in the ministry of the Word at that church. The procession glided in dance movement to the sound of traditional African music. The lectionary was presented to the celebrant who blessed it and returned it to them. They then proceeded to the ambo and 'proclaimed' the readings. There was a similar procession for the offering of the gifts of bread and wine. There was a further procession after Communion where those who could afford to do so, brought gifts which were to be distributed among the poor. It all added up to a very joyful but quite reverent celebration of the Eucharist.

Presence of Christ
Our Sunday Eucharist is first of all a gathering of the local Christian community. As such it presumes that there is some sense that those who gather actually form a community. Unfortunately, that sense of community is not always there, especially in large urban centres. My experience tells me that there is a significant difference in celebrating the Eucharist in a small rural community and celebrating in a large urban area where the sense of community may not be as strong. Gathering regularly for the Eucharist should help to create

and nourish that sense of community. The Eucharist is the sacrament of our union with Christ – we make up the body of Christ. Christ is present with us as a gathering who have come to pray together: 'where two or three come together in my name I am there with them' (Mt 18:20 GNB).

When we gather, we begin by acknowledging our sinfulness and we ask for forgiveness in the Penitential Rite. We move then to the Liturgy of the Word. We normally have three readings. The first reading is usually from the Old Testament, the second from the New Testament writings of St Paul and others, and the third reading from one of the four gospels. It is in and through the readings that God speaks to us, that God is present to us. In the homily that follows, the celebrant reflects on the readings, trying to discern how they might apply to his own life, and through that reflection, how they might apply to the lives of others. The homily is not meant as a lecture, it is not a scholarly analysis of the readings. It is, rather, an attempt to give meaning to what God is saying to us at this particular time in our lives. It is not meant for moralising or condemnation.

The homily is followed by the Profession of Faith which is a statement of the doctrinal teaching of the Church. There follows the Prayers of the Faithful which, as the title indicates, are prayers asking God to listen to the needs of his people both local and universal.

The heart of the Eucharist

The central part of our Eucharistic celebration comprises of the Offertory and the Eucharistic Prayer. We present the gifts of bread and wine which will become the body and blood of Christ. The words of offering both the bread and the wine refer to each as gifts from God and 'the work of human hands', reminding us that these gifts are our offering and, therefore, represent us and all that we do.

We then pray to the Lord to 'make holy these gifts so that they may become the body and blood of our Lord Jesus Christ'. The celebrating priest, acting in the name of Christ, recalls the happening at the last supper when:

> He himself took bread, and giving you thanks, he said
> the blessing, broke the bread and gave it to his
> disciples.

He repeats the actual words of Christ saying:

> Take this all of you and eat of it,
> for this is my body which will be given up for you.

Again he says that he took the chalice and once more giving thanks, he said the blessing and gave it to his disciples, saying:

> Take this, all of you, and drink from it
> for this is the chalice of my blood,
> the blood of the new and eternal covenant,
> which will be poured out for you and for many
> for the forgiveness of sins.
> Do this in memory of me.

The people are invited to proclaim their faith that Christ is present with them, as he was at the last supper and as he was in his death and resurrection.

'Mystery of faith' is the faith or belief that Christ is present under the appearance of bread and wine. We as a community gather regularly to 'do this in memory' of him, believing that in doing it in memory of him, it is not just a remembrance ceremony but acknowledgment that Christ is present now, with us, under the appearance of bread and wine.

Pope John Paul II used to speak of 'Eucharistic amazement' when reflecting on the mystery of Christ's presence in the Eucharist. In his encyclical on the Eucharist, he speaks of his hopes to rekindle this Eucharistic amazement by contemplating the face of Christ wherever he manifests himself, but above all in the living sacrament of his body and blood. He suggests that this amazement should always fill those who are assembled for the Eucharist and especially the priest who leads the celebration. While it is difficult, if not well-nigh impossible, to feel that sense of amazement each time we go on the altar, it certainly is a worthy ideal for us to try to keep before our minds.

Search for understanding
Thousands of books have been written, countless lectures have been given, explaining, exploring and trying to give some insight into and understanding of how Christ can be really present under the appearance of bread and wine. Of course we cannot explain; it is a mystery of faith. Two things strike me in that search for understanding:

- I sometimes worry about the way we speak of the bread being changed into the body of Christ and the wine being changed into the blood of Christ and the eating of flesh and the drinking of blood. We need to remind ourselves that we are talking about the sacramental presence – real, yes, but not real in the sense of material/physical presence.

We are receiving, welcoming, uniting in a unique way with Christ.

- My second concern is that we priests, especially in our seminary training, spent so much time analysing the nature of Christ's presence in the Eucharist that we got caught up in distinguishing between the philosophical concepts of substance and accidents, saying that the accidents of the bread and wine remained unchanged, but the substance of the bread and wine was changed into the body and blood of Christ. In a conversation with a bishop colleague of the Church of Ireland some years ago, I asked him about his belief in regard to the Eucharist. His reply was simply 'I am satisfied that Christ is present; the exact nature of that presence I just don't know.' It sounded reasonable to me and I trust that in saying that I am not in any way questioning or diminishing the true reality of Christ's presence at the Eucharist.

In a talk that was given in our diocese a number of years ago, the priest speaker reflected particularly on the words of consecration. This man's thoughtful reflections impressed me greatly and I have tried to apply his insights to my own understanding.

He took bread and gave you thanks

The Eucharist is of course the great prayer of thanksgiving of our Church. The very word 'eucharist' means thanks or giving thanks. The Eucharistic prayer begins with the preface: 'Let us give thanks to the Lord, our God – it is right to give him thanks and praise.' All of us have much to be thankful for: gratitude for the gift of life itself, for the gifts of food, shelter and clothing, of priesthood and religious life, of marriage and children, of friendship and love. What in life is not a gift?

He broke the bread
In the Jewish tradition, the breaking of bread for those present is the function of the head of the family. Traditionally it was the father of the family who broke the bread and distributed it. The action reminds us that God the Father is the giver of all good gifts. Distributing the bread and sharing it creates family and community. Sharing in the Eucharist creates and nourishes the Christian community.

The breaking of bread reminds us that Christ's own body was broken by his death. We are broken by our own sinfulness, by our failure to live up to our Christian ideals, by failures in charity towards each other, the broken people we meet, failures in justice by not challenging unjust practices, failures in chastity by ignoring appropriate boundaries, broken by scandals revealed in recent years, broken by illness, by death of a loved one, by an unhappy marriage, by unemployment and by the struggle to make ends meet. The Eucharist is a place to bring our brokenness to unite it with the brokenness of Christ.

Brokenness can become a real grace, enabling us to identify and empathise with the brokenness of others and thus become a source of comfort, of healing and of hope for them.

Gave it to his disciples
Christ gave himself to us in the Eucharist in a most intimate way. For priests and religious our very decision to enter priesthood or religious life was about giving our lives for the

service of others. In marriage the spouses give themselves totally to each other in love.

Do this in memory of me

The disciples could hardly have understood the deeper meaning of what was happening when Jesus spoke these words at their final meal together. That fuller understanding could only have come through the events that followed – his death and resurrection, the post-resurrection appearances and the coming of the Holy Spirit. It is clear, however, that they came to the belief that when they gathered together in prayer to do this in memory of him, they were making present again the mystery of Christ's death and resurrection. Through these gatherings, the Church was being birthed as 'they gathered frequently as a group, together with the women and with Mary, the Mother of Jesus and with his brothers' (Acts 1:14 GNB). As new members joined them 'they spent their time in learning from the apostles, taking part in the fellowship and sharing in the fellowship meals and the prayers' (Acts 2:42 GNB). For more than two thousand years Christians have gathered to do this in memory of him, believing that in so doing, they are again making present / re-enacting the death and resurrection of Christ. 'We proclaim your death, O Lord, and profess your resurrection until you come again.'

It is easy to analyse the richness in each phrase used but it is difficult, if not impossible, to give time to reflect on the phrases during the actual celebration. It would be a pity, however, if we just run off the words without thinking of what we are doing or saying. I used to sometimes say to priests that we should try to 'pray the Mass' rather than 'say the Mass'. Trying to mean what we say helps us to say what we mean and vice versa.

The Mass is not ended

At the end of the Eucharistic Prayer we move to the Rite of Communion. We begin with the Our Father which is very much a community prayer. We have the prayers for peace and the sign of peace. We move to the distribution of Communion in which we share in the body and blood of Christ. Receiving Communion is of course a very special and sacred experience for all of us. It is a very intimate and private experience and, at the same time, a communal experience. The very word 'communion' itself speaks of community.

The Mass doesn't end on our receiving Holy Communion. The celebration ends with the final prayer and the dismissal 'The Mass is ended, go in peace'. I am sometimes tempted to say 'the Mass is *not* ended, go in peace to serve the Lord and each other'. The Mass or Eucharist is incomplete if it does not make any difference to our lives. Gathering with our community each Sunday, believing that Christ is with us as we do so and believing that 'he who eats my flesh and drinks my blood abides in me and I in him', must surely make a difference to our lives.

Some years ago, I visited three of our diocesan priests who were working in South America. I was very impressed by the work they were doing among the poorest of people. I was even more impressed when they took me to meet Sr Peg O Rourke, a native of Milltown Malbay, who had been living in the very poorest part of a shanty town in Lima for fifteen years. Her home was a little galvanised shack with no electricity, no running water, no toilet – just a hole in the ground which was moved periodically in the tiny patch of ground beside the shack. As we talked, I, in my naivety, asked her, 'Do you miss being able to get Mass regularly?' She smiled, held out her hand towards the surrounding shacks and said, 'There is my Mass.' I didn't reply – how could I? Sr Peg had reminded me that the occasional Mass was sufficient for her because her Mass never ended. Her words so impressed me that I try to bring such an awareness to my celebration of every Mass ever since. Sr Peg taught me the lesson that indeed no Mass is ever ended but is always beginning in our daily living.

Spirituality of Communion

The Vatican II insight that the Church is the communion of the baptised is often overlooked. This is a pity as it gives a strong emphasis to the unity of all Christians, which calls us and challenges us to be united with each other and to care for our brothers and sisters. John Paul II, in his encyclical *At the beginning of the new millennium,* speaks of the 'Spirituality of Communion'. This involves regular reflection on the mystery of the Trinity dwelling within us and trying to see that same mystery in the face of our brothers and sisters as united with us in the mystical body of Christ. This unity with them enables me to see their gifts and talents as a gift from God, not only for them but also as 'gift for me'. In turn, my gifts and talents are not just gifts for me, but also 'gifts for them'. This spirituality inspires us to share our gifts and use them not just for ourselves, but for those around us. At times this may be very difficult, but that does not mean we stop striving in our efforts. Such striving should be at the heart of any vibrant local parish or Church community. We can have all the committees and councils, ministries and service, but if we do not continuously try to have a solid spiritual base to all that work, it will be in vain. This solid spiritual base must be a deep respect for each other which is, in turn, based on the belief that the face of God shines in each one of us.

Celibacy and access to Eucharist

There are many parts of the world where people are left without the Eucharist because of the lack of priests. Is the retention of celibacy in such cases more important than having a priest to celebrate the Eucharist?

It is with some hesitation that I risk saying something about compulsory celibacy for priests, yet it would be an avoidance of a very important issue not to do so. In what is known as the Latin (Western) Rite Church (the Church we grew up in) all candidates for ordination to diaconate – one year before ordination to priesthood – make a vow to live a celibate life. It is important to note here that celibacy and priesthood are not essentially linked. In the early Church, having married clergy was normal. Even in recent years we have had an increasing number of married priests in the Latin Church. Some have been Anglican ministers already married, who decided that they wish to become Catholic priests. Other Anglican ministers have joined the Ordinariate, set up by Benedict XVI to accommodate Anglican priests and those of their flock who wished to move with them to the Catholic Church. Many of those joining the Ordinariate have resigned from their positions within the Church of England because of the decision of the Anglican Communion to ordain women as bishops. The Eastern Rite Church (Orthodox Churches), which is in communion with Rome, ordains married men as priests – but if they are ordained first, they are not allowed to marry and are expected to remain celibate.

It is very difficult to establish a rationale for compulsory celibacy. To want to marry is a natural desire for the vast majority of people. We believe that marriage is sacred, that it is the foundation of a healthy and wholesome society. Some would argue that we cannot adequately minister in an understanding and empathetic way to married families unless we are married ourselves. It is really impossible to understand celibacy unless we see it in the context of faith. The Church sees celibacy as a commitment to serve, with an undivided heart, the kingdom of God:

> Called to consecrate themselves with an undivided heart to the Lord ... they give themselves entirely to God and to men. Celibacy is a sign of this new life to the service of which the Church's minister is consecrated; accepted with a joyous heart celibacy radiantly proclaims the Reign of God (*Catechism of the Catholic Church*, n. 1579).

Seen in that light of faith, celibacy can make sense as a generous gift to God. The reality is that many of us priests do not always see it in the light of faith. I think of several seminarians in my time who were very good candidates for priesthood but felt unable to undertake the celibate life and left the seminary. I have known several good priests who left the priesthood because they felt unable to continue the life of celibacy. I have no doubt that there are some priests still in ministry who find celibacy an enormous burden, which makes it very difficult to live a wholesome, joyous life.

In my own experience I have, at times, found it a heavy

burden, but I have no idea how life might have worked out had I been married. I believe that for those who are able to live their celibacy in a generous way in the service of the people, their priesthood is enhanced. For those who are unable to live it in that way, it can be too heavy a burden and makes us isolated and resentful.

Pope Francis, speaking to priests and bishops in Italy, talked of a sterile celibacy leading to bitterness and resentment and lack of fruitfulness. 'The key to a fruitful life', he said, 'lies in a double fidelity and double transcendence: being faithful to God and seeking him in prayer, remembering that he is the faithful one and opening oneself to others with empathy and patience.'

So, is there a solution to the issue? I believe that any attempt to suppress discussion of the matter is no solution. I don't have any answers either, but I believe that we need to have enough faith in the guidance of the Holy Spirit to examine other possible options. I am not convinced that celibacy should be abandoned. I am satisfied that it is a very important charism that has served our Church, our priesthood and our people well. I simply ask the following questions:

- Could the vow of celibacy be replaced with a promise of celibacy for a specific number of years with the option of taking a solemn vow of celibacy at the end of that period?

- Could it be agreed with a man leaving priesthood to get married that if he wishes to return to priesthood after a specific number of years, his application would be formally considered?

- Could it be possible that married men be ordained in order to provide the Eucharist in places where people are, at present, unable to have it because of the lack of priests?

- Without any intention or desire to provoke controversy, is there any link between celibacy and how women are seen and treated in the Church?

$$\text{---} \quad 17 \quad \text{---}$$

Being Human and Christian

Sacredness of our humanity

When we think about religion and about Christianity we tend to think of something that is outside ourselves. We think in terms of God, Jesus Christ and perhaps the sacraments. We seldom think about our own humanity when thinking of religion or if we do, we often see our being human as an obstacle to our Christian living. Being human was not something those of my generation were taught to rejoice in. We tended to be taught how to cope with our humanity and even how to control our humanity. It was as though our humanity was a threat to our Christian living. And yet we often pay tribute to a religious person by saying that he/she is very human. We appear to be saying that despite being religious they haven't allowed religion to destroy their humanity.

There is nothing wrong with being human. That is what I am, that is who I am, that is how God has made me, and so in his love he must surely rejoice in my humanity. God did, after all, choose 'to share in our humanity'. Being human ought not to be a burden but a joy.

Let's look at it this way: let's begin where we all began in the form of a newborn child. The birth of a child brings great joy to parents and to extended family and friends. The presence of a newborn touches all hearts and, in most cases, drives away the fears and doubts that may have existed when the pregnancy was first confirmed, as well as strengthening the resolve to meet all challenges and fears and to do the best for this new child. The innocence, the utter dependency of a baby – its helplessness and vulnerability – seem to bring out a joy that melts all hearts. We celebrate a baby's birth as representing so much of the positive of what all human life is about. A newborn is human life manifested in all its glory of faith, hope and love. We herald human life with one response only – joy in our hearts.

And the wonder and the joy and the love that surrounds the newborn child is in keeping with our belief that we are created in the image of God; that you and I are a product of God's creative love in and through the love of our parents. Our parents, godparents and siblings may not have expressed it thus at our births, but we can be sure that they participated in their own way in that common denominator that is joy at the beginning of a new human life. Our births, yours and mine, were surrounded by that sense of joy.

Nowadays, we of an older generation can almost envy young adults who grew up with an awareness of the joy felt about their births. Their parents are freer in talking about emotions and feelings. They will have told their children all about how wanted they were and what joy their coming into the world brought to their parents and families. It is a great start in life and throughout life to have all the self-confidence that comes from knowing you were loved and wanted long before you were born.

Fearing our humanity

As the child grows towards adulthood we learn that life is not always full of joy. While we rightly rejoice in our humanity, we are mindful that as humans we are limited. We are not gods, we are free to choose right and wrong and we know that we are capable of doing wrong. But I feel that my generation were in some way afraid to be human. We felt we needed to control our humanity and not allow it to lead us to sin. Those of us who were studying in seminaries were often challenged with the gospel invitation, 'Be perfect, therefore, as your heavenly Father is perfect' (Mt 5:48 NRSV) – a tall order! We were given the impression that unless we were perfect or near to being perfect we were not fit for priesthood or religious life. Deep down we knew we were not at all perfect because of our weaknesses. Still, I had the impression that others were much nearer to being perfect than I was.

For many of us, that sense of failure to live up to the ideals set before us gave us guilt feelings, lack of confidence and something of a tendency to self-denigration. We didn't allow ourselves to be human, didn't allow ourselves to recognise and to accept our own vulnerability. Much of the emphasis was on controlling our humanity – does anybody remember the phrase 'predominant passion' and the unspoken impression, in my mind anyhow, that it was linked to my sexuality? The dangerous human tendencies towards pride, covetousness, lust, gluttony, anger, envy, and sloth seemed to get more attention than the grace-filled fruits of the Spirit – love, joy, peace, patience, kindness, gentleness, faithfulness and self-control. We feared our humanity which could lead us to sin, rather than rejoicing in our humanity which could lead us to generosity, forgiveness and love. Maybe it is a question of achieving the right balance between the awareness of all that is good in our humanity and in human activity and the need to exercise discipline in relation to our weaknesses.

Recognising and accepting our humanity

Weakness and failure are part of the human condition. Recognising and accepting our own sinfulness, our own vulnerability enables us to empathise with others who are vulnerable and broken in their lives. Recognising and accepting our own weakness also helps us to recognise the need for the saving power of Christ in our lives. Accepting and recognising our own weakness should not, however, leave us burdened with guilt, with self-denigration and with lack of belief in our own value and goodness.

Accepting and living out all that is best in our humanity can at times be confusing, untidy and uncertain. There is a real attraction to adopting a clear set of rules to avoid this uncertainty. Such a set of rules and regulations can give a sense of security and, indeed, can serve us well in disciplining our lives. We need, however, to clearly understand that rigid adherence to a set of human rules must never be used to set aside the basic principles of justice, of compassion and love. We sometimes find that rigid observance of a set of rules can become more important than the values which inspire them and can lead to that religious fundamentalism which appears to be gaining ground among many faiths today, including Catholicism. This fundamentalism can eventually lead to terrible injustices in regard to individual freedom, minority groups and particularly, in some societies, the debasing of women. On a human level, we can be fearful of feelings and emotions. I worked with a priest in our diocese who I admired a great deal. He was my boss for a number of years and I haven't worked under a kinder or more considerate boss. A group of us were talking one day about priesthood and the question was raised about 'job satisfaction'. His immediate response was that 'job satisfaction' should not be a consideration. Doing our work as priests was a duty. Getting satisfaction from carrying out our duties was quite irrelevant.

How much of what we do is done out of a sense of duty: it is part of my job; it is expected of me; people will be annoyed if I don't do it? How much of it is done because it is the natural human thing to do and to do it with a sense of joy and satisfaction? So often I feel that my training has put an ideal up there and that I will always fall short of that ideal. Can I not just see being fully human as the ideal and rejoice in my being fully human?

Sexuality and vows of celibacy

Reflecting on our humanity must include the subject of sexuality and sexual relationships. Obviously, being a male committed to live a celibate life limits my ability to fully understand the wider area of sexuality and sexual intimacy. What I say on this arises from my own experience of sexuality, from reading and from discussion with other people. Hopefully, it will make some sense to fellow priests and religious and help others not vowed to celibacy to gain some understanding of how one person sees and interprets this commitment.

We all have a need and longing for human intimacy. Each one of us is in a different place with regard to our sexuality because each of us has had different experiences in our lives.

Some of us may have had difficult experiences in childhood which have had a very significant impact on our sexuality

I believe that the deepest human intimacy we can achieve is the full, loving sexual intimacy between two people committed to each other in a permanent loving relationship. We, as priests and religious, have committed ourselves to live a life without such loving sexual intimacy. We have committed our mind, body and spirit primarily to service of God and of people. Our Church has discerned that an appropriate aspect of the expression of this commitment is the foregoing of sexual intimacy. The vow or promise to live a celibate life is not just about renouncing sexual intimacy and it certainly is not about ruling out other forms of human intimacy; it is about offering our lives to God in the generous service of people.

As I offer the following thoughts regarding our commitment to celibacy, I make no to claim to any expertise or training in the area and even at eighty-one years of age, I am still trying to improve my understanding of my own sexuality.

The commitment to celibacy obviously does not free us from desires for sexual pleasure, whether through partial or full sexual intimacy or through sexual fantasy. These desires can, at times, be very powerful within us. It is deeply wrong to sexually exploit another person, which we can do if we treat them as object for our pleasure without regard for their emotional state. But it is tragic for ourselves if we so fear our sexuality that we put a hard shell around it to prevent any danger arising from it.

To love at all is to be vulnerable. Love anything and your heart will certainly be wrung, if not broken. If you want to make sure of keeping it intact, you must give your heart to no-one … It will not be broken; it will become unbreakable, impenetrable, irredeemable (C. S. Lewis, *The Four Loves*, 1960, p. 11).

To refuse to love is to deny our humanity.

It is very likely that at some stage, or indeed at several stages in our lives, we will meet and get to know someone towards whom we feel a strong sexual attraction. If the attraction is reciprocated then we need to be aware of the appropriate boundaries and to exercise discipline in that regard. If we do so, then the experience can be enriching and can develop into a very healthy and rewarding friendship. If we fail to exercise that necessary discipline, it can have enormous implications for both people involved and can result in very serious long-term hurt. Married people are not immune from this sexual attraction to another person either, and also have to be conscious of appropriate boundaries.

We live in a world which is highly sexualised through various media – television, internet, printed word, fashion and commerce. We can become drawn into the fantasies offered by the internet especially, and become trapped in that world. Pornography makes objects of people and is a distortion of sexuality. For those not fully at ease with their own sexuality, it can become a very unhealthy addiction. This danger applies to everyone and not just clergy and religious.

I believe that celibacy, if and when we are able to live it generously, is a precious gift which we offer to God and the people whom we serve. If we are unable, or fail, to live it in a generous and loving way, it can become a very heavy burden and can contribute to us being lonely, isolated and guilt-ridden. I suspect that very few of us fit neatly into either category mentioned here. Most of us are probably somewhere in between, but struggling to live it as generously as possible.

It is important to avoid becoming obsessed with our sexuality – either with sexual attraction to another person, or sexual fantasies. While our sexuality is fundamental to our being, integrating it fully with the whole person we are is a healthy way to live it. Then we neither deny our sexuality, nor allow it to dominate our thoughts and actions. We commit our body, mind and spirit to the service of God and of people.

No human person can totally satisfy all our emotional needs. Those of us who have vows of celibacy can sometimes have romantic ideas about the wonder of sexual intimacy enjoyed by married people. We can feel frustrated and even bitter that we have been denied such happiness. But of course, those who are married can also be sometimes frustrated and unhappy because their partner has not fulfilled their hopes and dreams of complete happiness. We are not gods; no human being can fulfil all the hopes and dreams of another human being.

Our sexuality is part of that total gift of life given to us by God. It is part of our humanity, part of who we are. It is, therefore, something sacred and precious. If we treat it as sacred and precious, it will enhance and enrich our humanity. If we misuse it, it will damage us and demean us. Worse still, we will damage and demean other people who are equally precious in God's sight.

Humanity of Christ
Christ in taking human form, in sharing in our humanity, gives testimony to its sacredness. And Christ truly shared in

our humanity. I sometimes feel that our belief that Christ was both human and divine in some way diminishes our conviction that he was fully human. We suspect that it must have been easier for him to cope with his human limitations because he had the back-up of being divine. But such an understanding would surely diminish his humanity. In fact, some scripture scholars today suggest that the human Christ who journeyed through his earthly life was not aware of his divinity. But whatever the truth is in this regard, it is clear from the gospels that Christ lived a fully human life with all that that implies. He was born a helpless child, totally dependent on his parents, Mary and Joseph. It is reasonable to presume that as he grew up in their care, he joined the neighbouring children in their ordinary activities.

Our first glimpse of him as an adult is his going down to the Jordan to hear and to be baptised by John the Baptist. Something special happened there when he sensed that he had a special mission from God. He immediately goes to the wilderness where he is tempted to use his power – 'if you are the Son of God' – to do things that are beyond our human capacities. He rejects the invitation to turn stones to bread when he is hungry or to demonstrate his powers by throwing himself from the pinnacle of the temple without hurting himself, or to hasten his mission as Messiah by taking over the leadership of the world. He responded to all three temptations, presenting himself as a human person with all the limitations which that implies. He simply trusts in God without any expectation that God might intervene in any miraculous way. Throughout his public life he shared the human limitations to which all of us are subject, but lived his humanity to the full. He experienced joy and sorrow, courage and fear, energy and tiredness, anger and serenity. Perhaps it was most of all in his Passion, beginning with the agony in the garden of Gethsemane and ending with his death on the cross, that the humanity of Christ is most striking.

In Gethsemane he is overcome by fear of what was likely to happen to him. 'Grief and anguish came over him' and he said, 'the sorrow in my heart is so great that it almost crushes me.' And he prayed, 'My Father, if it is possible take this cup of suffering from me. Yet not what I want, but what you want' (Mt 26:36–39 GNB). And later on the cross he presents as on the verge of despair, 'My God, my God why did you abandon me' (Mt 27:46 GNB).

Jesus, by being fully human, dignified and sanctified our humanity. It is important that we recognise and appreciate the goodness and the sacredness of our humanity and of the myriad in actions that we do on a daily basis – the friendly greeting, the work in the home or in the workplace, the care for the young and the old, the sick and the lonely. Goodness is not confined to prayer, to Church or to sacrament. All that we do in our lives in an open, honest and generous way is good and sacred.

We have been given our human life by God. Our humanity is sacred and something to rejoice in rather than to fear. Jesus said, 'I came that you may have life and have it to the full' (Jn 10:10 GNB). Our goal should be to achieve and enjoy such fullness of life.

~~ 18 ~~

A Grateful Heart

Transforming misfortune into blessing

My friend Padraig died a few years ago at the great age of
ninety-six. He was just eighty when I first met him. We
quickly became very good friends despite it being unusual to
make new friends at our age. He was a man who carried the
wisdom of his years lightly. One of the characteristics that I
found particularly attractive in him was his capacity to turn
misfortunes, or what most of us would call misfortunes, into
blessings. He told me a story about how he had been accepted
for a job at one time, but a person in a higher position
interfered, without any justification, and the job was given to
someone else. I think I would have been bitter about the
injustice, but not Padraig. 'I went back and continued in my
old job and, as a result, I met Mairéad and we had a good life
together.' He moved from Dublin to Ennis after Mariand
died. He was away from his house for a couple of days and
when he returned he found it had been broken into. 'Did you
find that upsetting?' I asked.

'Not at all, it was the neighbours who broke in because
they missed me.'

'Did you see that as an intrusion into your privacy?'

221

'No, no! in fact it gave me a sense of security – my neighbours cared.'

Padraig wasn't into complaining – he saw the refusal of the job ultimately as a blessing and was grateful for that. He saw the invasion of his privacy by neighbours as a sign that they cared for him. Padraig had the habit of counting his blessings rather than storing up hurts. He had a grateful heart.

Some psychologists tell us that a spirit of gratitude is something that some people acquire early in life and others do not, and that we cannot alter that spirit later in life. It's a case of once grateful always grateful, and once ungrateful always ungrateful! Whilst not questioning their expertise, that rigid characterising of people into grateful and ungrateful seems to me to be too black and white. I would like to think we can nurture and nourish a sense of gratitude and thus improve our behaviour in this regard. Gratitude is part and parcel of being Christian and as such can be taught and presented to people as an ideal towards which we can strive.

Gratitude in the scriptures
Certainly, the scriptures are not found wanting as a source of inspiration for the spirit of gratitude. They have a continuous stream of expressions of gratitude to God for all his blessings. Many of the Psalms are songs of thanks and praise to God. 'Give thanks to the Lord for he is good and his love is eternal' (Ps 117 GNB); 'All things the Lord has made bless the Lord: give glory and eternal praise to him' (Dan 3:51–90 NJB) and the canticle continues on to praise God for the sun, the moon, the wind and rain.

When we move to the New Testament, immediately we have a hymn of praise and thanksgiving from Mary in the Magnificat: 'My soul magnifies the Lord ...'(Lk 1:46–55 NRSV). This is followed by Zachary's hymn of praise at the birth of John the Baptist: 'Blessed be the Lord, God of Israel' (Lk 1:68–79 NJB).

Jesus' own life was characterised by a spirit of gratitude. He presents as constantly being aware of God's loving care. He speaks of Abba as a loving father with whom he enjoys deep intimacy. He sees the Father's love as enfolding the world and all that happens in that world.

Why worry about clothes? Look how the wild flowers grow; they do not work or make clothes for themselves. But I tell you that not even King Solomon with all his wealth had clothes as beautiful as one of these flowers. It is God who clothes the wild grass – grass that is there today and gone tomorrow ... won't he be all the more sure to clothe you (Mt 6:28–30 GNB).

He is conscious that everything is a gift from the loving Father and he was deeply grateful for that: 'Father, Lord of heaven and earth. I thank you because you have shown to the unlearned what you have hidden from the wise and the learned' (Lk 10:21 GNB). Because he sees the Father's loving care for all creation, it is reasonable to assume that there were prayers of thanks when he was alone praying to his Father.

At the most solemn moment at the last supper, Jesus took a piece of bread, gave a prayer of thanks, broke it and gave it to his disciples, 'Take and eat it,' he said. 'This is my body.' Then he took a cup gave thanks to God and gave it to his disciples saying, 'This is my blood.' Then he said, 'Do this in memory of me.' The early Christians, interpreting the will of Christ, saw the Eucharist as the great prayer of thanksgiving – the very word 'eucharist' itself comes from the Greek and means thankful.

Again, Jesus saw a spirit of gratitude as the appropriate response to gifts received. When he healed the ten lepers he expressed his disappointment that only one of them returned to give thanks. 'There were ten who were healed, where are the other nine? Why is it this foreigner is the only one who came back to give thanks to God?' (Lk 17:17–18 GNB). He was critical of the lack of gratitude in the parable of the unforgiving servant. The master had forgiven the servant for a very large debt. This servant went away and found a fellow servant who owed him a very small sum and when this servant pleaded inability to pay he had him thrown into prison. Jesus condemns the unjust servant, saying, 'You should have had mercy for your fellow servant just as I had shown mercy on you. The king was very angry and sent the servant to jail' (Mt 18:33–34 GNB).

On the other hand, he clearly appreciated and praised the woman 'who was a sinner' for her appreciation of and gratitude for his forgiveness of her sins. Indeed, he contrasts her generous loving behaviour with that of more formal but less loving approach of Simon the Pharisee who had invited him for dinner (Lk 7:36–50).

Nurturing a spirit of gratitude
The early Christians were exhorted to give thanks to God for all their blessings.

Thanks be to God for his inexpressible gift (2 Cor 9:15 NRSV).

And whatever you do in word or in deed, do everything in the name of the Lord Jesus giving thanks to God the Father through him (Col 3:17 NRSV).

Give thanks in all circumstances; for this is the will of God in Christ Jesus, for you (1 Thess 5:18 NRSV).

I referred earlier to the fact that psychologists tell us that a spirit of gratitude is something that is acquired at an early age and that it is very difficult to change that spirit later in life. While that may be true to some extent, I do believe that that spirit can be nurtured and developed even in people in whom it had been neglected in earlier years. It is the old nature versus nurture debate again. I believe that all of us can improve in our appreciation of and gratitude for the gifts we have been given.

Gratitude is a Christian ideal and, as with all such ideals, transforming grace can have an effect on our sense of gratitude. One of the most effective ways of nurturing and indeed transforming our spirit of gratitude is surely our prayer life. If we try to make a habit of regularly thanking God for the good things in our lives, we will nourish our sense of gratitude for all the gifts we have received. We can praise and thank the Lord for the gift of life itself, for the gift of food and shelter, for the gift of health, the gift of friendship and love, the gift of faith and Eucharist – the list is endless.

Perhaps the real test of our prayers of thanks is that we give thanks not only for our own gifts, but also the gifts given to others. If we can rejoice and give thanks for the gifts of others, then we truly have a grateful heart. The Pharisee in the parable, who gave thanks that he was not like the rest of men, was really praising himself rather than God to whom we owe our gifts. Equally, thanking God that I have enough food when others do not, or thanking him that I am forgiving when others are not, is hardly the prayer of a grateful heart. Of course, I can give thanks to God for the food I eat provided there is a real concern for those without food. If my prayer of thanks is to be transforming, then it must have the effect of wanting to share my gifts with others. A truly grateful heart is also a generous heart.

I mentioned earlier Pope John Paul II's encyclical *At the beginning of the new millennium*, where he talks about 'spirituality of communion'. This spirituality of communion enables us to share the joys and sorrows of our brothers and sisters, to sense their desires and attend to their needs. It enables us to see what is positive in others, to welcome it and prize it as a gift from God. Equally, I would then see that my gifts are not only gifts for me but also gifts for others to be shared with them. It seems to me that the 'spirituality of communion' is the spirituality of a grateful heart.

Whatever about the nature versus nurture debate or the spirituality of communion, all of us admire people who have a real sense of gratitude in their lives. Some time ago, I wrote a short article for a magazine. Soon afterwards, I got a letter that really touched me. The writer was a woman who in recent years had lost her husband and a son, the latter in tragic circumstances. She spoke of both with obvious deep affection and with palpable grief. She then went on to thank me for the article and to thank God for all the good things in her life. I was quite moved on reading it. Here was a woman who had suffered a great deal and yet retained a sense of gratitude for all the good things in her life. If I were in her position, would I be grateful for my blessings or would I be angry, or even bitter with God, for the loss of my husband and son?

On the other hand, it saddens me when I meet people who appear to be incapable of counting their blessings, who only seem able to count their troubles. I accept that life can be very difficult for some people and I just don't know how I would cope if I were faced with a terrible family tragedy, with permanent ill health or the collapse of a business.

I find it very inspiring to see the manner in which some people faced with difficulties can still retain the capacity to be grateful for their blessings. I find it hard to understand people who always seem to focus on minor inconvenience and who seem completely unaware of all the good things they have in their lives. Is it that in our Western society we have lost the capacity to count our blessings and to be grateful for what we have?

Some years ago, I had the privilege of visiting some priests of our diocese of Killaloe who were working amidst the poverty-stricken people in the shanty towns around the city of Lima in Peru. I can honestly say that I encountered far more smiling faces in those shanty towns than I ever see walking the streets in an Irish town. Amidst the poverty, they appear to have the capacity to be happy today as long as they have enough to eat. They appear to have the capacity to enjoy and to have a sense of gratitude in relation to their lives.

I note a comment of Pope Francis: 'I can say that the most beautiful and natural expressions of joy which I have seen in my life were in the poor people who have nothing to hold on to' (*Evangelii Gaudium*, n. 7).

Is our relentless pursuit of material things destroying our capacity to enjoy the present moment? No sooner have we got what we wanted than we begin again to think about what we now need. We can easily get trapped in the much-wants-more syndrome and consequently we are always wanting.

A grateful heart is a praying heart and so I will end on a prayer:

Thank you, Lord, for all the blessings you have given me especially the gift of life itself, the gift of friendship and love. May I always see these gifts as a gift, not just for me, but a gift to be shared with my brothers and sisters.

19

Growing Old

Retirement

I was looking at cards recently for a friend who was celebrating his sixtieth birthday. The caption on one of them read: 'When the good years are over the better ones begin.' I am not sure that all of us would agree that the better years are the years when the bones begin to creak, when the glasses you have searched for are on you and when you are not sure whether it is Mary or Patricia, even though you have known Geraldine for years! Growing old does present its difficulties but it also brings its blessings and its opportunities.

For most of us, the first significant factor in reminding us that we are growing old is our retirement. For some, retirement can be a quite traumatic experience. To have gone to work every day for forty years and to suddenly find oneself with no good reason to get out of bed in the morning can be difficult. Life can appear to be without purpose; the friendships, the camaraderie, the banter of the workplace are suddenly no more. The phone doesn't ring, the emails and letters cease – except for the bills – and one's sense of import-ance is taken away. And you realise that the world doesn't stop when you get off. The job you have been doing has been taken on by a younger person who has more up-to-date skills and competence.

For others, retirement can be quite liberating. At eighty-one years and now restored to good health, I am satisfied that these older years are proving quite enjoyable. Having generally worked hard as both priest and bishop for some fifty years, I am finding the more relaxed life of retirement a very pleasant experience. Yes, I sometimes miss the more fulfilling aspects of the work. It seems to me that growing old – with the good health proviso – can be a very enjoyable stage of life. I see – with a little envy at times – the joy of grandparents in the lives of their grandchildren. I continue to be a member of a seniors' choir and it is proving to be very enjoyable, even though I always had the impression that I couldn't sing. Some of my fellow choristers may think that I still can't sing. The requirement for membership, however, is not that you can sing but rather that you are old enough! There is a great sense of camaraderie in the choir and some people who organise entertainment events have the impression that our singing prowess adds to these occasions! It takes a little courage to join a new club. We are all hesitant in putting ourselves forward but most clubs are very welcoming once we take the first step of joining.

Letting go
I have always liked that lovely piece of scripture at the end of John's Gospel:

> When you were young
> you put on your own belt
> and walked where you liked;
> but when you are old you

will stretch out your hands,
and somebody else
will put a belt around you
and take you
where you would rather not go (Jn 21:18 NJB).

Sometimes we experience that sense of someone taking us where we do not want to go. Old age is challenging for the individual. It is a challenging time too for his/her family, friends and carers. During my own illness I found family and friends extraordinarily kind and supportive. At times, however, I felt that some of them in their concern were inclined to prematurely put a belt around me and take me where I didn't want to go. All of us as we grow older want to keep our independence as long as we possibly can. I truly think that at times families can be too eager to decide what is in the best interests of the older person without actually listening to the person him/herself.

As I grow older I am enjoying doing the gradual unpacking of this new phase of life for myself. It can be hard to allow ourselves to be led, to lose our independence, to be taken where we do not want to go. And yet there are, or will be, times when we will have to let go. Letting go is an essential part of growing old, but only when it's called for. I like to think that, in common with many older people, I appreciate the concern and efforts of my family and my friends to help and support me in a realistic, non-intrusive manner.

Most parents as they grow older will have to let go of their children. I can only imagine that such letting go can be a very difficult experience for them. They will have seen their children in whom they have invested so much of their life and love now sharing that love with some other person or persons. They may also have to accept that their children may have chosen a way of living that is in conflict with what they, as parents, would have hoped for. They may find that they have to accept that some of those whom their sons or daughters have chosen as life partners are not always to their liking.

Another part of letting go may be the questioning of some of what we thought were the certainties of our faith, which formerly stood us in good stead. It is not easy to admit to oneself or to others that you are not so sure any longer about the very beliefs and values on which you have based your life. At this stage of life I am finding that I can live with these uncertainties and just simply trust in the Lord that he lovingly understands our difficulties.

As we grow older we need to try to let go of any hurts there may be in our lives. Holding onto hurts only increases the feeling of hurt and delays the process of healing. The same applies to letting go of regrets. All of us, at various times in our lives, have regrets about things we have done or things we have failed to do. Of course we have all failed, at times, to live up to the ideals that we inherited from our parents and would have set out for ourselves earlier in life. Failure is part of the human condition. Of course we have made mistakes. But our God is a loving and forgiving God, so I shouldn't need to worry about mistakes of the past.

There are lots of 'might have beens,' like choosing a different way of life. Wouldn't it be lovely to have married, have had children and now have the joy of grandchildren in my old age? But would life have been happier if I had chosen a different path? All I can say at this point is that priesthood has been kind to me. Yes, there were ups and downs, there were times of joy and of sorrow, and there were successes and failures, though how success or failure in priesthood is judged is hard to decide but I am happy at this stage to have chosen priesthood as a way of life. I have a sense of gratitude towards the Lord and towards the people who influenced me to follow the path of priesthood.

Perhaps the most difficult letting go in our older years is letting go of people, especially people whom I have known and loved over the years, be they family or close friends. Ultimately, all of us will be faced with our own letting go of life itself. While the idea of letting go of life may seem very frightening, my experience over the years in being with people when they were dying has been generally reassuring.

Letting go is never easy, whether it is of power, possessions, family or friends or even of life itself, but we don't have a choice in this regard. (I am reminded of the interested party who enquired how much did Jack leave and was very wisely told that 'he left everything'.) We need as we grow old to accept and acknowledge that we too will leave everything, so let's leave everything in the Lord's hands.

Caring for ourselves

As we grow older there is a danger that we begin to neglect ourselves. Perhaps we feel that we are coming towards the end of life and that caring for ourselves is no longer important. Maybe it is because we have no one who will draw attention to our negligence. Possibly there is a feeling that no one else cares about us now, so why should we be bothered about these things anymore. But I believe that caring for ourselves is a sign of respect for self and others as well as appreciation of our own dignity.

We need to care for our physical well-being. We need to eat properly, take suitable exercise – such as a regular daily walk – and enough rest when needed. Something that is not often spoken about but which is a risk for older people who live alone is a gradual dependence on alcohol. Sometimes the nightcap or the glass of wine with a meal, both of which are very pleasant, can steadily increase in quantity. The ability of alcohol to temporarily dull the edges of loneliness, pain, regret and sorrow can make a growing dependence on it develop almost unnoticed.

We need to care for our emotional well-being. When I studied philosophy we spoke of man and woman being a 'rational animal'. But to interpret the word 'rational' as simply being capable of intellectual reasoning is to impoverish ourselves. We are not just rational in that narrow sense, we are also relational. Being capable and comfortable in relating to others is an essential quality of normal living. As we get older, it might be more of an effort to stay involved in things, or to become involved in new and different things, but it is an effort worth making. We cannot live alone in this world. I don't know if there are some people for whom the security of God's love is sufficient, but if there are such people I believe they are few in number. For the rest of us, we need to relate to some small number of people in a loving and caring way. Part of that relationship is to allow others to know me fully – and that's a risk. It's a risk I'm willing to take because I value close friendships.

We need to care for our intellectual and spiritual welfare. By this I am thinking of the need to continue to nourish ourselves with prayer and reading as we grow older. I was never a great reader and I am conscious of that deficiency. I have always been more at home with either physical activity or listening and talking to people. Good spiritual reading helps the prayer life. We will have different tastes in reading, and different writers will appeal at different times, but I think this kind of reading helps both our minds and souls – even if we tend to fall asleep with the book in our hands!

Our body, mind and spirit, our very lives are gifts from God. I believe it is important that we appreciate these gifts, take care of them, nourish them and bring them to full fruit insofar as we are capable of doing so. I like what the Dominican Timothy Radcliffe says: 'We grow old well when we let God's grace work within us as a perpetual renewal, childlike to the end.'

I have a strong conviction that as we grow older, the God whom many of us were taught to fear in our earlier years has become a God who is kind, compassionate and loving. It is against that belief that I lay aside any regrets, ask forgiveness for my failures and happily leave my future in God's hands.